CASUALTIES OF LOVE AND LIFE

ALEXIS QUINTIA ODEN

Library of Congress Control Number: 2025917697

ISBN: 979-8-9994441-4-1 (Paperback)
Imprint: Quintiassential Ink Press

ISBN: 979-8-9994441-5-8 (Hardback)
Imprint: Quintiassential Ink Press

Dedication

This book is dedicated to my late great nephew, Jasiah Anthony Dudley. You are the inspiration behind my decision to get my poetry out to the public. In your four short years here on Earth, you have motivated me to live with a purpose, just as you did daily. I love you past death. You are a true angel amongst us.

I want to thank the Lord for providing me with this beautiful talent so that I may use this ability to share my thoughts and feelings with the world. Without you there would be no me. Thanks for giving me life, protecting me, and guiding me through such a harsh world.

Also, a special thanks to my friends and family who have supported and encouraged me throughout the years.

Dear Reader,

Casualties of Love and Life is a tribute to everyone who is just living everyday life and trying their best to succeed. My subject matter is extremely versatile, so everyone will be able to relate to my themes. This is a collection of the private poetry I have created over the last thirty years. These poems are inspired by my personal situations and those of friends, family, strangers, and/or loved ones throughout my life. I've met many different people throughout the years, while moving around often, growing up as a military dependent. I have been able to sit back and observe how various situations have played out in other people's lives, as well as my own. This poetry book embodies my thoughts, feelings, experiences, and opinions. This is not an autobiography. All poems are not centered on myself but are merely my take on love and life in this world from diverse points of view, both observed and imagined.

Some pieces explore hope, faith, and renewal, while others address sensitive themes such as abuse, loss, addiction, or social struggles. *These poems are shared as reflections and creative expression, not as professional, medical, or legal advice.* If you are facing such challenges, I encourage you to seek comfort and support from trusted resources. My intention is not to provide answers, but to offer reminders that even in hardship, light still exists.

Some poems address sensitive themes that may be triggering for certain readers. Reader discretion is advised.

CONTENTS

CASUALTIES OF LIFE

Preface

Casualties of Love and Life - We have all been victims of love and heartbreak derived from the endless situations we place our hearts in. And we have all survived. Sometimes we are the innocent bystanders; sometimes the ones toting the gun shooting the bullet into our loved one's heart. We also fall victim to life – not allowing ourselves to succeed because we are afraid of failure, falling victim to circumstance, or becoming statistics of the poverty or dysfunction we were born into. Some of us were dealt worse hands than others, but it is a dog-eat-dog world and you can either sink or swim in this game of love and life. Choose to survive and thrive. The good news is – you can find redemption in the smallest things, and rise again, with faith. Many people will choose the easy route, cutting corners to succeed, but I am a firm believer that you cannot cheat your way to triumph. Everybody has a choice. The foundation must be sturdy, and from this, you can fly.

The title of this collection came to me after losing my four-year-old nephew. At that time, I felt like a casualty of just living life, because I was still alive, but constantly beaten down with bad news. He passed on and I was left behind, struggling with survivor's remorse. It is devastating that he did not get a chance to live a full life. But he is in a better place now, a place where he is not suffering. We on earth are the ones in worse shape. We must live and learn to love again, creating our own heaven on earth.

People die, kill, rape, and children are born with incurable diseases. It's inexplicable and heartless, but when we recognize how to be resilient, with positivity, we rise. We're told that we live in the land of the free, but it seems as if we are often fighting for our freedom in our daily lives. We are living in a battlefield, even without stepping outside of our own homes. It's time to step into our power, take control, be proud, and rise in love and faith.

These poems touch on many contemporary subjects, inspiring us to be better people, to think before making decisions that make us *Casualties of Love and Life* – and instead, to survive and thrive.

Note

This collection represents the author's personal reflections and creative expression. Some poems address sensitive topics such as abuse, loss, addiction, or social issues and give voice to personal feelings or to experiences observed in others. These works are not intended as factual accounts or as professional advice. Any resemblance to actual persons, events, or circumstances is coincidental. This work is not associated with, nor does it reflect, any organization, agency, or institution.

Author's Note

This collection spans many years of my life. Some poems were written in adulthood with a mature voice, while others were created in my teenage years when my writing was raw and unfiltered. These youthful works reflect emotion and urgency more than literal accounts, and I include them because they mark the foundation of my journey as a poet.

Pieces such as *Awaiting Death or Prison, Prisoner's Song, Hunting Season, Words Hurt Too, My Psyche, Missing Cycle, Unborn, Robbed, Heartbroken, Back Shots, Safe Place, Fast Lane,* and others—found mostly in Part 2—explore themes of social pain, raw emotion, faith, regret, survival, struggle, and at times, references to self-harm or violence. These works arise from lived experience, imagination, and observation, but they are not literal accounts. Such references are metaphorical and artistic in nature, written as imagery rather than instruction or advocacy. They are not intended as condemnation of any group or system, nor as endorsement of harmful acts. Rather, they serve as testimony to resilience and growth—a reminder that even in hardship, hope can still rise.

PART 1:
CASUALTIES OF LOVE

Good Die Young

Dear God, tell me why do the good people always die?
And why is it that the bad ones still have their lives?
This is hard for me to understand
But I know that with you, my family is in good hands.

It is so erratic how life changes in an instant
I never met anyone as gifted, even as an infant
Jasiah, you have changed my life for the best
The doctors said you wouldn't take a first breath
But you did, you were blessed!

For four years strong, you proved them all wrong
I can't accept that you're gone
Your memory will forever live on
But God had to take His angel back home.

The worst thing was watching you leave
It's difficult for me to breathe
Just knowing that you are not here with me
I'm still in disbelief!

Why didn't God just take me instead?
There are so many thoughts running through my head
God, there is so much he didn't get a chance to see in this world
Why did he have to leave?
He was my whole world!

I can accept it when the glove fits
But when it doesn't fit, then it doesn't make sense
I am sorry for questioning you
I'm just so confused.

There are rapists and murderers that are still loose
So, why choose to take my nephew?

A mother shouldn't have to bury her kids
Why do the good die young, and the bad ones live?
Forgive me for trying to find reason
He went in there with a smile, and he came out not breathing
This can't sink in— I won't believe it!

That moment I will never forget
Or the pain of telling the kids
That I could never forget!
That smile, I will forever miss
In my heart, he will forever live
I will give anything to have him back.
I will give anything to hear that laugh.

Doctors aren't supposed to make people worse
No family should have to feel this hurt
I'm grateful for him because he saved my fam
We were at a low point and God gave us him
There are still some things that I will never understand
But I know that God has a plan.

IN LOVING
MEMORY
OF

Jasiah Anthony
Dudley

God's Child

People always want to know
How I can be so young with a mature soul
For I take the lead and I will never follow
They want to know, why I have such a gracious glow
Because I'm not just beautiful from the outside, but it's also internal
For I walk the road less traveled
I blaze my own trails with God's light
That's how I shine so bright.

I learned at a young age
That popularity won't get you into Heaven's gates.
You can't buy love or respect for that matter
So, it's not about who got there faster
But how you climbed that ladder
It's not about how nice my hair is laid
It's not about my pretty looks, or my thin waist
That is not what leaves everyone amazed
It's all about my faith
Because I walked with the Lord the whole way.

It's not just my beauty, but my brains
The fact that no matter what obstacles I face
My Lord will always keep me safe.
He protects me, when the world neglects me
When friends abandon me, there he'll be.
I don't need diamond rings
Or all the finer things that life can bring
My Father Lord is all I need
Without him there'd be no me.

I will never give into the pressures of my peers
He takes away my doubts and fears.

So, when I look in the mirror, a strong woman appears.
With His love, I can conquer it all
With His love, I feel ten feet tall
There's no one above Him, He's the one I love
You can't tear me down, because He has built me up.
So, when you feel alone and scared
Just remember God is always there.
I am God's child, and I say it loud
I am God's child, and I say it proud.

It's Over

What's going on? What's gone wrong?
My heart is beating rapidly, what am I to do?
I can't accept that I'm losing you
Deep breaths are going out and in
I can't believe this is happening
I thought it was you and me
I thought we were meant to be
I thought it was us against the world
But, I guess I shouldn't think.

They say if you believe it, then you can achieve it
Well I believed in us
And I thought we were in love
I thought I knew who you were
But now you're with her
And I'm so hurt because we're over.

I done reached the mountain peak
I done crossed the deepest sea
And I'm still in disbelief that it's over between you and me
I really can't believe that it's over
I need some closure
I thought I was your ride or die
We were the new Bonnie and Clyde
I thought I was your soldier.

I was shocked when you said you were in love with her
And you know what's worst is that I introduced you and her
Why am I so hurt?
Is this what I deserve?
My best friend with my boyfriend, that's betrayal to the fullest
My mama always said, "Don't hold on to what can't be kept."

In the back of my head, I knew that we wouldn't last
But I loved you so bad
I gave you everything that I had
And I guess I was playing make-believe
Because now you're telling me there's no you and me.

I wish I would have known this
Before I invested my soul and my heart in you
Now I'm so confused, what am I to do?
I felt it in my bones, and now I'm all alone
I thought you were the one for me, but now I'm feeling so dumb.
Never again, will I play myself
Never again, will I love a man more than I love myself
Please help me, I'm thinking back like what the hell?

I am constantly blaming myself
I keep acting as if it's me
But there is nothing you can do to stop a man from being a cheat
No matter how well he gets treated
If he wants to, then there is nothing you can do
I thought I knew who you were
But now look at us
The man I met no longer exists
And now you're telling me that it's over.

Best Drug

There's nothing like being able to release yourself on someone
Sex is fun, but nothing tops being in love
That electric connection you feel in that moment
Knowing that it's yours, and you own it
When you can see your name on it
The heat and the chemistry
There's no feeling so deep
No high greater to peak
There's nothing like being next to your soulmate
There's no greater feeling in the world
Than letting someone so closely inside your intimate space
A conversation without words, embraced in a strong hug
The best drug is making love.

Ice Box

There is no more pain for me to endure anymore
For I am so cold, I have an icebox where my heart is stored
You can put a torch to my chest, but it won't melt
And you can give me your heart, but it won't help
It is way beyond frozen; no heat can make it thaw
Not even if I stood next to the sun, I've tried it all.

I'm just in the state of mind where I need to find myself
And it's unfair to you to hold onto something that can't be kept.
If I had one wish I'd make myself whole
But he took half of my soul and I just can't let it go
You can take what's left of me, but it's not much
That's like grabbing a rainbow – you can't touch.

I'm barely breathing
I'm sleeping, one eye open
I'm constantly losing focus
I refuse to relive that
You remind me of the past
This is what happens when a good woman has gone bad.

I'm damaged goods, why would you want to deal with that?
It's a losing battle, why would you want to play scrabble?
You're at war with my heart, and it's torn into parts
I never thought that I would fall, and I fell hard
Not just cuts and bruises, but wounds and scars
I'm trying hard, but I can't go far with a glacial heart.

Keep Lying

I'm tired of being home alone
I'm tired of going through your phone
I'm tired of these games you play
I'm tired of feeling this way.

Lying won't get you nowhere, you got to be honest with me
Lying won't get you nowhere, but out on your butt and lonely
You say you love me, but all you tell me are lies
If you loved me, you wouldn't be wasting my time
If you can't love me right, someone else will
If you can't treat me right, then I'm out of here.

Because you keep lying, like you're trying, but you're not
And I keep crying, man these tears won't stop
What do I have to do, to get through to you?
How can I prove, that I'm all for you?
What do I have to do to make you see?
Everything you need, is all in me.

I can't let you waste my time, telling me lies
It's not going to change, it's still the same
My heart says stay, my brain says walk away
I need to get over you, get under someone new
Tired of being played for a fool, tired of waiting on you
When you're only going to continue to keep lying.

These tears, they won't stop coming down
They won't stop
These tears, they won't stop pouring down
They won't stop
As long as you keep lying.

Cocoon

Living here in this cold world, I'm always putting up a fight
But inside there is an insecure little girl waiting to go outside
I see the light, and I often wonder
To take the road less traveled, I ponder
But you're so far away.
I can't keep my pace; it feels like I'm going to break.
Lead the way, with you I feel so safe
I can't face the pain; you keep me dry in the rain.

Spread your wings and close your eyes
Free that little girl that's inside
Face your fears because they all must die
You must spread your wings and fly.
Soon you'll bloom, my butterfly
When it's time you'll soar so high
Just spread your wings and fly.

When you're by my side, I get the strength to rise
When I'm on my own, I don't know how to fly
I'm just a cocoon not ready to come alive
But one day I will rise on my own and soar so high.
I know I must break away, so I can fly away and grow
It will be challenging without you, but I must go on my own.

Making My Way Back to You

Goodbye. That was the last word I said to you
Before I left you blue
After you told me you loved me, I said I loved you too
But I know that only made you even more confused.
Now those words heard over the phone linger in my ear
As I visualize us on the porch, my dark clouds become clear.
You make me feel beautiful, you make me feel safe
When I'm lost and insecure, you give me that faith.
You're the best thing that's happened to me
You could never be replaced.

I look at myself in the mirror each day, it's so painful for me to face
And pride is so hard to swallow; it leaves such a bitter taste.
I had to face my skeletons, and I had to do it alone
I got trapped and caught up, so I must make right out of wrong.
I must learn to love myself, before I can love anyone else.
I had to put my needs first,
There were so many questions unanswered,
I needed to research.

I feel with love I've been cursed
And I need to find myself before it gets worse
I finally understand why everyone around me gets hurt
Because I've been so naive
To think that pleasing others while lying to myself could work.
Only you see my potential, no one else has, not even I
And I drown myself in tears each night
Because I can hear your heart cry
And it's screaming out to me
"Come home please!"

I know what it means to say I love you, baby, I do
Even though it may seem like my brain is missing a few screws
And it kills me knowing all this agony and torture I put you through
But the truth is I'm just beyond confused
I wish I could be strong like you
And not be afraid.
I wish I could care less about what others say
I wish I could just toughen up and be brave
I know you've had better days, I'm just so ashamed
Before me, I bet your life was simpler and free of half this pain.

Leaving you was both my best and worst mistake
My best, because now I'm finding my own way
I'm finding who I am in such a dark place.
My worst, because I can't take being away
I put so much at stake
And it's unfair for you to have to wait
We're meant to be, because it's fate
But the best things in life aren't a piece of cake
I want to give you the whole me, but majority of me is missing
And I refuse to come home to you in this poor condition.
I'm trapped between love, life, and being a Christian
My heart says one thing, but my mind just won't listen.

There were so many obstacles coming at me all at once
I hated the person I was becoming
I felt like I was slipping away from God, and I was being punished
Just knowing I disappointed you makes me sick to my stomach
I'm getting stronger each day to become the woman you wanted
I'm not worthy of your love
At this point you deserve more than what I can offer up
How can I love you, but betray your trust?
How can I lie to you, and leave you crushed?
Now I'm staring at these four walls and it sucks
I just want to lie next to you and feel your touch
I don't blame you if you moved on and given up
Just more work I must put in for when I fight for us.

When I'm at my best, I will make up for time lost
Because we'll be together forever, no matter the cost
I couldn't ask for anything more
But because of my deceit, I've ruined all we stand for
I must live with the guilt that I let you down
And if you give me another chance, forever we'd be bound
I told you once not to sell me short, but I've done that on my own
Once I'm better, I'd make it up to you
And I'll promise to never leave you alone.

I must focus, and sort my life out
But I have no regrets of being with you, and certainly no doubts.
I know it's difficult to believe I'm gone
But I miss you, and soon I'll be home
I'm conflicted, depressed, not knowing where I belong
Emotionally breaking down, but I need you to be strong
I don't want to burden you with any of my fears
You're everywhere; I see your face inside my tears.

If loving you is wrong, I don't want to be right
But I'm kidding myself thinking I can be so naive in life
I've been living in two worlds, and it's been exposed
Karma creeps up in strange forms
Even when you think your past is closed
The pressure, stress, and guilt are eating away at me
I feel drained, fighting for love while questioning every belief
I'm locked in balls and chains; I'm trying to be set free
I am fighting my inner self currently
While making my way back to the person I breathe.

Sullen Cries

Where did you go?
I've searched Heaven and beyond to find you, but still no trace
I figured I'd go home and you would reappear
But I was just left with an empty place
And a lonely embrace
So many mixed emotions, but love conquers them all
Before you I was conniving, selfish, and lost
But I wouldn't change this love for anything in the universe
Even though now I'm balled up, crying, so hurt.

I thought I could move along
But I can't because everything reminds me of you
It's like my whole life is in high speed, and I can't think, I just do
I wish I could stop this, but it's beyond my control
It's like something has empowered my body,
and it just won't let go
I can't work, I can't eat, and I can't sleep
Without you I'm empty, lonely, and weak
These are the confessions of me
Inside I'm very hollow
And I pass time drowning my sorrows with liquor in a brown bottle.

I must be strong for the kids, but they see right through it
Why did you have to leave me with a broken heart and ruined?
I don't understand, it was supposed to be us
Coming out to the public, and defending our love
But you bailed out on me
Even though you told me you were ready, and you were so happy
Now I'm stuck in confusion, and I'm depressed, what happened?

I thought you'd be the one to bring me to pure joy and ecstasy
But ever since we been together, it's been pain, lies, and grief.

And yes, the good outweighs the bad
But my heart only reads inconsistent beats.
Please, tell me what is wrong? What it is about me?
That make every lover I meet want to leave
I thought this was different; I was honest and gave you my all
Ok, I get you needed space— but you couldn't even call?
Do you know the pain you put me through,
the agony and the worry?
I was at my highest high, now I'm at my lowest low
And my vision is now so blurry.

It used to be we'd tell each other everything;
there were no secrets at all
You're my best friend and lover, we were inseparable
Wherever there was you, there was me
Now, I'm alone with shattered dreams
I'm barely able to breathe
Just waiting impatiently, for you to return home to me
But I still have no regrets, because you were my best
Now I'm so in need
And still I continue to soak my sorrows; I'm scared and misty blue
How can I fight for two without you?

We felt whole together, but now you made us a fraction
We're supposed to be hand in hand, and you're missing in action
You left me alone in this war
Not even knowing if you're still a part of the battle
I got faith that you still want me, but your actions leave me rattled
We can take on the world together, but I need you by my side
It takes two to make this work, so how much longer do you hide?
I breathe you!
Every time the phone rings, in hope and despair,
I say your name aloud
And over time, I look around,
and I swear I visualize your face in the crowds.
Do you see what you're doing to me?
Whatever it is, we can deal with it together,
I'm here through anything.

You're my most important person, did you forget?
Let me remind you, and help you understand this
We're both confused, it's not easy, but nothing worthwhile is
But, if you want something bad enough, then you go get it
This is not me, I never been the one to chase
I feel like a complete fool, pathetic, and so out of place
We have a family, and there was a lot at stake
I wish you could have just confided in me,
before you just ran away
I got some intense news today, and I needed your comfort
It's difficult to handle bad news when you're a loner
The kids miss you as well
Through my forced smiles they have seen me suffer
It's just hard to believe you are gone, knowing how much I loved you.

Long Distance

You're incredible, precious, amazing
It kills me dead, you're my craving
And when I can't go on you're my motivation.

I just envision you staring me down, with those sexy eyes of brown
You make me happier
I forget the reason I was sad, because when I'm with you,
nothing even matters
You're my world; the man I love and adore
And it's hard to walk away when I feel you in my core.

I'm dying internally, I feel like shutting down
And I can't deny my emptiness since you left town
Damn, I'm going insane; you are the only thing on my brain
Life without you just is not the same
I need you here to rid my pain.

When two people love each other,
They just should not be kept apart.
We have been through too much,
For us to just go back to the start.
I know you can hear this no matter how far you are
Because even in absence we're still in each other's hearts
Half of my soul is missing, and it's difficult for me to focus
I hold your picture next to my heart
Because there is where you feel the closest.

Let Go

I have to let you go
It hurts to see her touch you, a beautiful smile lit on your face
It's painful to know another woman is making you feel this way
A frown hid behind a smile
Only thinking what could have happened, if you and I got down.

But you're content now, so I just need to let it go.
It's hard to watch it all unfold beneath my nose.
It's like a moth to a flame, so intense—
but that's the way love goes.
I gave my all, but she's who you chose.
And she's a great woman, so I should just fold.

I try to move on, but nobody's like you
I got to get in a 12-step program, because I'm feeling so misty blue
The wedding is coming up soon and it will be tough
But I'm pleased that you're happy, and that's got to be enough.

You and I are forbidden, and it pains me deep
But if I lost you as my best friend, it would just kill me
Faded pictures in a broken glass
Or is it just illusions of what we could have had?
Well that's something I'll never know
But the one thing that I do know is I have to let you go.

I Can't Help It

We have been dating for a little bit, our three-month mark is today
You're trying to get closer, but I can't help but to feel this way
The things that you do, and the things that you say
Have me feeling like everything is going to be okay
But in the back of my mind, it just goes in rewind
Wondering if you'll just cheat and lie
Or if you're just wasting my time
Are you going to hit and run like most guys?
I can't help but to think that is all you want
I can't leave my heart open, just to get it broken.

I can't help but to think, that you're going to play me like he did
I can't help but to think, that you have ulterior motives
I can't help but to think, that all men are just the same
I can't help but to think, that you're just playing games
I can't help it.

I'm living in the past; I'm so used to crying
So, it's weird for me to laugh, because inside I'm dying
I want to be happy, but forever I've been sad
You two are so opposite, you treat me so well,
and he's treated me so bad.

I can't feel pleasure, when all I know is pain
It's like telling the sun to shine, in a place that only rains
How do I change, when I feel so afraid?
I feel like every move I make, will only be a mistake.

I won't be the one, checking messages on your phone
I won't be the one, always suspecting that you're doing me wrong
I won't be the one, thinking you're cheating when you're not in sight
I won't be the one, waiting up late at night and starting fights.

I can't be the girl, that's so insecure and so hurt
I can't be the girl, always thinking that you're doing the worst
I can't be the girl, always trying to dig up some dirt
I want to be with you, but I need to work on myself first.
I won't be that girl again.

New Beginnings

It's the unknown that has me confused
Like a traveler embarking on a path brand new
Not knowing which route to choose
Feels like a chess game, I hope I make the right move.
I never connected with another so quick
You swept me off my feet, our chemistry was so intense
I met a lot of players and dogs,
And toads and frogs,
In this search for my prince
No sideline games, I don't sit the bench.

When I first met you, I knew you were special
And my heart skipped beats at your sight
Frozen in time, like a deer caught in headlights
I craved you some nights
Often wondering what your touch felt like
Your skin against mine
Your chest against my breast
While feeling your soft caress.

Imagining the taste of your lips, against my lips –
in a sensuous kiss
Stricken by infatuated bliss
A fantasy turned reality I wished
But at the time you had a girlfriend
So, my feelings were on the backburner
And ever since then, time has never been in our corner.
Maybe we will get a chance to get to know each other better
I barely even know you, but it feels like I've known you forever
But— only time will tell.

Damaged Property

I can't believe he did a number on me
Now I'm stamped damaged property
But he won't get the best of me.

I know you're not him, you are someone new
But I am not ready to make those moves
So really it is me, not you
Never again will I play the fool
It's not fair for you to stand accused
For what the last man did before you.

I need to move forward
But I get flashbacks of how he did me wrong
When a good girl has gone bad
It's a wrap, she's completely gone
And there is nothing like a woman scorned.

It's a pattern that won't end
She gets hurt, so she hurts him
Then it starts all over again.

Breaking Point

My love has a limit, I'm so sick of it
How long did you think that I'd put up with this?
I was the best you ever had; How can you upgrade from that?
I was stupid and foolish, to think you would make me your wife
I can't accept that it came to this, I've invested 3 years of my life
But I can't teach an old dog to do new tricks.

I can't believe, that you have me feeling like Kelis
I hate you so much right now!
Deuces up, peace— I am out!
You won't get the best of me
I devoted everything, and I gave you all of me
The world wasn't enough for you, you wanted galaxies
Just save me the excuses please
And just pack your things and leave
To the left, to the left
You lost your best, but now I'm on to the next.

I can't concentrate
I am at the point that I am about to break
I can't take any more pain and heartache
Something has got to give, because I can't keep feeling this way
There is no more that I can tolerate
We needed a better way to communicate.

You kept pushing me away, but now I am done
You needed to man up, but I guess you weren't man enough
You kept testing my love— over and over
And pinching my last nerve
This goes out to every girl in the world
Especially for colored girls.

No Change

Lately, it feels like all we do is fuss and fight
We are constantly breaking up to make up
Then it's right back to the break ups
No love, it seems like it went away
No touch, we seem so far away
I can't get it back
I want to get it back
But it's too late.

You won't change, and I won't change
Same old things, nothing changed
So, it is best that we go our separate ways.

Baby, I know that it's going to hurt
But, we could never ever make this work
Believe me if I could, change things for us, I would
But, it's just not fair, holding onto what is not there
It's going to be hard for me, but I know I must leave
Ladies, can you feel me?
Fellas, can you hear me?
I see no changing, there is just a bunch of complaining
There is no compromise, just sleepless nights
And it won't get any better, if we were to stay together.

You won't change, and I won't change
Same old things, nothing changed
So, it is best that we go our separate ways.

Guess Not

How do you go to Hamburger Helper, when you had steak?
3 years down the drain, seems our whole relationship was fake.
How could you tell me that you love me, and then lie to my face?
I got your whole life in my hands, just cry me a lake.

You would diss me for your boys;
I could have sworn y'all had a thing.
I was the perfect girlfriend—
bought your clothes, cooked, and cleaned.
You stayed broke, so it wasn't about your green.
The way I was addicted,
you'd swear I was a crack fiend.

Who drove you around when you fell of your feet?
And even though your son is not mine, he calls me mommy
Who took the blame when you had two strikes?
Who stood by your side when you got into fist fights?
I found phone numbers from Keisha, April, Tiffany, Alize'
It takes a weak woman to stay, but a strong one to walk away
So, I'm taking what's mine, and leaving you behind.

I'm not going to lie, I do miss you
But, the hand we were dealt was critical
Somewhere down the line the feelings changed
I was drowning in pain, and couldn't stand the rain.

Flashbacks of how you caressed my body
That was then, and this is now, I have somebody
I saw you the other day, and we caught eye contact
But that was the past, this is the future, and I can't go back.

Our Saving Grace

You were an angel on earth
The doctors said you wouldn't make it to birth
Oh, how you proved them wrong
Four years strong, and you continued to hold on
They counted you out, but the Lord counted you in
Now He came back to retrieve you
Because He needed you with him.

You were so young with a mature soul
You are my inspiration, my hero
I've learned more in life from a four-year-old
Than any teacher has ever taught
When all odds were stacked against you
You pushed forward and fought.

My little superman, warm heart with a helping hand
That sweet, angelic smile and beautiful laughter of yours
I will forever remember
You are my sunshine in the winter
Our miracle baby, my first nephew
What did I do to be blessed with someone as wonderful as you?
Such a beautiful spirit inside and out
When God made you, He was showing out.

I know you are in Heaven looking down on us
We'll be strong, so you can be proud of us
No matter my mood, you always kept a smile on my face
I have comfort knowing you are in a better place
In my heart you could never be replaced
I'm still in disbelief
How could this be, when you are my everything?
Lovable, fearless and brave, you rescued us in so many ways
You will always be in our hearts, you are our Saving Grace.

Insanity

It's been five years to the day
You took my hand, and said be my baby
Steaming hot then, now it's freezing cold
And these games you're playing, they're getting old.

We keep doing the wrong things twice
Expecting it to come out right
Just going back and forth
Expecting different results
But he will never change
That man there, he's still the same.

I keep on believing the hype
That you're going to make me your wife
Then ten years will fly by, and I'll be asking myself, why?
Now I realized, he was just wasting my time.

It's insanity every time I go back to him
I keep doing the same things expecting different outcomes
Five years we've been together
Had our ups and downs, but is it getting better?

No ring on my finger, marriage won't happen it seems
It's time for me to move on to better things
Once I let go then I can begin to become whole
There are plenty of fish in the sea, so I'm throwing out the tadpoles.

Heartbroken

When I walked in I expected you to be sleeping
Never once did I imagine you creeping on me
I told you when we first met
I was not one to play
Now my life is damaged, all because of one heartbroken mistake
As I'm sitting here in this chair
Electric about to fry my brain
I still don't regret the fact, because of me,
you're turning in your grave
Well say hello to your mistress
Or maybe I'll tell her myself
Because, as soon as they pull this switch,
then I'm going to see you both in Hell.

A poetic reflection on betrayal and pain. References to execution and revenge are metaphorical and creative in nature, not a literal act or endorsement of violence.

Damaged Goods

I wish I would have known you years ago,
before your life had changed
Before the first girl broke your heart, before you experienced pain
Before you doubted who you were, before you climaxed off rage
If I were your girl, in another world, your life wouldn't be the same.

I've looked into your eyes; I know you were delighted at a time
I've seen the good in you; I've seen you smile bright like sunshine
Everyone wants happiness, which you can't deny
In life you're scared to try, and for you it's easier to hide
I can't call it— something is draining you inside
And has stolen your will to survive.

If I were your first
You would have never experienced hurt
At least not of your heart being ripped out your chest
Because the one you thought you trusted the most
Wasn't looking out for your best.

Damaged goods that's what you are
When a good man's gone bad, he's permanently scarred
You used to have a heart of gold, but now it's so tarnished
It's nearly impossible to mend an angel who has fallen
So I won't, because a dog roams
But he will always find its way back home.

I'm where you should be
Every man needs a good woman behind him
Which even Ray Charles can see
All you've ever known was dysfunction
No happiness, just disloyalty, and no good loving
So, I don't blame you for giving up— it's just sad
Because you're missing out on the best thing you could have ever had.

Back Shots

I need love, so what do I have to do to get through to you?
My heart is on life support, and it is in critical
Cupid's arrows keep shooting but they keep on missing you
What do I have to prove?
Without you, there is nothing to lose.

Damn, I feel like a fool
These love blues got me so confused
We made mountains move, so anything is possible
We could have been so remarkable
I feel so exposed and so vulnerable
Now I'm all alone, I'm just so lost and gone
I am a ticking time bomb.

I feel like you put me through a head-on-head collision
And my heart took a fatal ending
It's bleeding out, these wounds cut too deep
I'm constantly lying in our bed sheets, singing sad karaoke.

These sullen cries and wishful tears, are just longing for you near
Each drop that appears, only manifest my fears
I'm dying internally; I need you next to me
Your back shots got me weak.

You shot me in the back—no warning, no chance.
My heart broke in two from the force of that glance.
Each jab left me weakened, unable to stand,
Stripped of my strength by life's cruel demand.
Those back shots haunt me, every scar they create,
Reminding me of love that turned into hate.

Lost at Sea

Even apart you're seducing every bit of me
Effortlessly, you're stomping on my heart critically
I promised myself that I would never fall this deep
I'm freezing, with no life jacket, just lost at sea
And baby, you're the only one that can save me
If loving you is wrong, just shame me
I must leave, because you're draining me.

You keep pulling me in like the sea, and taking control of me
You got me questioning all my beliefs
I was blind, but now I can see
I loved you whole heartedly
We could have been a masterpiece
But you took advantage of me
Now rapidly, I'm aiming at your heartbeats
You're going to feel every bit of pain as me.

First fact is to never hold on to what can't be kept
I put too much time into a loser, and that is what I regret.
I know we had our good times, I must admit it
But, when it's all finished, you're the reason why my wrist is slit
And the reason I wake up in cold sweats, gasping for breaths
I'm an emotional wreck, but what's next?

I have this heat in my lap, while I'm watching Snapped
I'm just plotting how I'm going to get you back
Because, when a woman is scorned— then it's a wrap!
I must get my life back on track
No more pretending that you loved me back.
Now I only see faded pictures in a cracked glass
But I'll have the last laugh!

This is the sound of my heartbreak
I'll show you pain and heartache.
I'm going insane, because I'm racking my brain,
Life without you is just not the same.
I'm going insane, with this heat to your brain,
If I can't have you, then no one else can.

These pieces (Back Shots and Lost at Sea) are symbolic expressions of heartbreak and emotional struggle. References to self-harm or violence are metaphorical, written as artistic imagery, not instruction or endorsement. They reflect creative expression, not literal accounts.

God's Love

He fills me up with His love
He protects me just because
Unlike these other men, I don't have to stroke His ego in return
He is genuinely concerned.
I remain drug free
Because He is all I need
I pray every day, He's so addictive
He knows all my secrets, and He always listens.

With Him it's so simple
I wear the purity ring because my body is my temple
We're a perfect fit, tight like a glove
And when I'm somber, He showers me with hugs
This is a connection nobody can touch
I'm glad my first love is the man up above.

Through it all, I am standing tall
You won't see me fall, because I got God in me
He's the perfect man, nobody can compete
He accepts and loves every part of me
He keeps me on my feet
He makes me strong when I feel weak.

You can go ahead and hate, but I'll just dust it off
With God by my side, haters are just a lost cause
With God in my life, I will never ever fall
With God in my heart, all I must do is call.
With His love I can be anything
For His love is why I sing.

He's in my corner every step of the way
He always keeps my whole family safe.

I know He is always holding my hand
I wouldn't be me without Him
So, when you feel like you just can't win
Just remember God is always your friend.

Permanent Exhale

How do you let go, when you're combined at the soul?
I'm losing control
Step back, because he really has a hold on me
I'm taking deep breaths
Finally, I can now breathe!

A feeling I never felt
I'm on permanent exhale
I loved you from day one
This is a feeling I couldn't escape from.

You make my heart smile
Too bad this feeling didn't last a while
Because the way you walked out was just so foul
I should have known, nothing can last eternally—
Not even a platinum ring.
So I'll just inhale—
Until you return to me.

Two Can Play

Those nights you went out, I was with him
I fell in love, and I didn't mean to hurt you, but I can't pretend.

Those nights you were with her, I was with him.
At first, I was being a good girl and staying in alone
Then I found out that you weren't on your own
So, two can play this game.

I wasn't going to stay home and wait for you to return
You were doing you for a while, so it was my turn
You used your best friend as your alibi
And swearing y'all were hanging out
But the joke is on you, because when you're gone,
He is at our house—so two can play this game.

I don't know how to say this, but I must make this clear
It's been a long time coming, and I must get out of here
I've been in denial thinking you're the one for me
So, in the process of doing me, I realize I must leave.

I can't keep doing this anymore
I can't keep going back and forth
I can't keep hurting inside
I can't keep in all these lies.
I'm done playing this game.

I'm moving on with your best friend
I'm leaving you and moving on with the best man
He treats me so much better than you do
I didn't mean to hurt you, but this is what's best for me to do
Don't act shocked, surprised, or all confused
You put me through the ringer, and left me abused.

Karma stepped up, because you get what you put in it
You took advantage of what we had, but now we are finished
You lost at your own game.

He was there to lift me up when I was hurt
He gave me everything I deserved
He showed me my own worth
All of this happened while you were with her
Sorry for the heartbreak, but my heart was on a quest
And I guess at your expense, I found love
So, I hope for your next woman's sake, that you learn
not to play games.

Complicated / Feelings

Is it that serious?
I can't eat or think without you running through my head
I try to fight the urge
But what I feel is unheard of.

Why am I stressing over you?
You're definitely not stressing over me.
Should I just forget it, and ignore my feelings?
Or should I give you all of me?
In hopes that you'll eventually love me too.
I know we're in two different places
But every time I see you my heart races.

Everything would be so simple if you weren't in my life
Ignore you is what I just can't seem to do right
Why must everything be so complicated?
Why are you what I'm always craving?

It's the feelings that leave us so emotional
I can't help that these feelings leave me so vulnerable
We can't live without them
And we wouldn't be human without them.
Love, hate, and everything in between
When all is up, here come the feelings.

Nothing Special

I used to think the world of you
I thought you were so wise
I thought you were loyal and unique, not like other guys
I knew there was something special about you
But now I see the truth
You revealed your disguise, now I see the real you.

I thought you were special
I thought you were the one
Your intensity, the way you devoured me
But I guess you're like that with everyone
I thought we had a connection
At least it seemed so from my point of view
But, I guess when you're alone, anything feels like home to you.

Five years of friendship went down the drain
Because we thought with private parts
We didn't bother using our brains
You said you'd make me fall in love
I fell hard, but you never picked me up
I went from complete to empty in a matter of seconds
And my friend was no longer there to clean up the wreckage
I once thought the world of you
But now I realize that you are nothing special
Because you got my hopes up, then twisted my heart like a pretzel.

Consolation

What do you get out of it?
Is there any thrill in being used and abused?
You get tossed like a bean bag from dude to dude
Going from bed to bed in search of love
But you're looking in all the wrong places
When will it be enough?

You're too quick to trust
And even quicker to give it up
You're in denial about what's really love and lust
And you can't even look yourself in the mirror
So, where's your consolation?
What do you get out of it?

You don't even know the worth of your treasure
A few minutes of pleasure
Doesn't equal up to the pain measured
I just don't understand it
Of course, he is getting his
But most of the times you don't finish when y'all have relations
So, where's your consolation?

The way I see is it, you get nothing at all
Not even a phone call
No ring or a prince, just a bunch of frogs
So, where's your consolation?
What do you get out of it?

Guardian Angel

Have you ever heard an angel sing?
Have you ever felt an angel's wings?
I have—and it was the most beautiful woman I've ever seen
And we called her Geraldine
But her name was Grandma to me.
She never let me fall
Always on my side like my shadow on the wall.

The queen of all queens
When I was on the edge, she pulled me back
I stay strapped but with no gat
Because she was my secret weapon
There is no question, she is my protection.

My guardian angel, I wish I was with you in Heaven
Wouldn't that be a blessing?
No more stressing, no more life's lessons
Ever since you left us, my heart has been reckless
But, I know that you protect us.
Grandma, you saved me, and you gave me new sight
When their stones grazed me, you protected my life.

Thankfully I'm still in one piece
You're the air that I breathe
Without you they'll be no me
I was blind, but you made me see
I still can't believe that the cancer intervened
Now I realize, not even death can come in between you and me.
I know you're in Heaven smiling down
I hope I still make you proud.

Soaring Waves

No one can be what you've been to me
The love we share can't be compared.
You're my sunshine on a rainy day
You're my board riding through the waves
Surf's up, and we're soaring high
Through the storms, and through all tides.

When I stare in the mirror, what do I see?
A strong individual, and that's how you made me
These haters can't make me weak
These haters won't ever break me
It's attention that they seek, so I'm turning the other cheek.

God made me this way, and they can't take that away
No matter what they say, you'll never break my faith
I'm down on bended knees, dear Lord please, come and rescue me
You always protected me, when the world neglected me.

I can't describe how I feel inside
He makes me happy and that I can't deny
He's the reason I sing, I don't need diamonds or rings
I got God in my life; He's all the man that I need.

Love's Pattern

What gives you the right to just leave her out in the cold?
Just left out in the cold...
Alone, freezing, with no one to hold.
She lusted you, she trusted you—
but did she really know?
Somewhere inside, she had to have known, right?

You used her, you abused her—
now she's lonely and abandoned.
Emotional wounds cut the deepest,
they never fade like scars on skin.
She'll nearly drown a few times just to learn how to swim.

Emotional abuse is the worst you can receive
Physically you heal, but inner wounds are deep.
She constantly sinks just to rise from this pool
She's scorned for life—because of you!
It's similar to how your ex did to you.

It's a pattern that never ends—
you get hurt, so you hurt her,
and then she hurts him.

Hunting Season

Reality will sink in
Just as I'm leaving
You'll realize, that I'm the best thing breathing
You got caught up cheating
What were you thinking?
But it's too late, you can't pick up the pieces
The rifles are out, and it's dog-hunt season.

It's dog-hunt season, dog-hunt season,
If your man is a dog, then unleash him
Ladies start packing up his stuff, because he's leaving
I'm spring cleaning
Getting rid of this dead weight, a new meaning
You are just a weakling
And justice I'm seeking
You left my heart leaking
Now, it's time for the reaping
No more tears, and no more weeping, not I
Big girls don't cry, we get even
So, it's time for the dog hunt season.

I hang my man up like a trophy
I hurt him like he hurt me
Ladies if your man is not treating you fair
And you just want to get him out of your hair
Line them up in a row
It's dog-hunt season, it's time to let him go.

This piece is a metaphorical expression of heartbreak and empowerment. References to violence are symbolic, written as artistic imagery, not instruction or endorsement. It reflects creative expression, not a literal account.

I Know

I'm just me, real and unique
Known to make toes quiver, and stop heart beats
Some climax just hearing me speak
I can see it in your eyes; I know that you want me
You want me, I know you do, how can you not?
I don't mean to sound full of myself, but how can I not?

I've proven to make you melt
My slightest touch sends chills down your back
I can take you to heights unimagined, how can you say no to that?
I'm unlike anything you have ever encountered
In fact, I bring out your best
And when the time comes there will be no regrets
Because I'll guarantee to conquer your greatest sex.

No one can compare
Yet you chose misery over happiness, bad over good?
What other woman do you know can treat you better than I could?
I've touched places you never knew existed
How can you say no to this?
I know when we're apart, I am missed
And I am definitely at the top of your wish list.

I've tickled your deepest thoughts
And replaced your past knowledge with doubts
I gave you reason to hope, and that's only half of what I am about
How can you cheat yourself? That is the question
I accepted your strengths and weakness; flaws and perfections
I can provide you with everything
I can fulfill all your wants and needs
But you chose to settle for the worst, when it's best that you
Just put faith in me.

Meant to Be

It's fear that I speak of, because I'm so afraid to lose myself
I am afraid that when it's all said and done,
I would only have myself.
I am afraid that if I don't stand up tall,
then I would just only fall short
But now I can see that you and me, we're destined to be,
like Kobe on the court.
Baby you light my torch.
Me without you is like no fireworks on July 4th.

You're meant to be in my life because God gave me a sign
I was blinded from what was staring me right in front of my eyes
Kept my feelings inside, convinced my mind otherwise
But the heart never lies.

Our vibe is unique, unlike anything else
Honesty that is so rare and pure like a chastity belt
I melt at the slightest touch of your lips
Rubbing against my lips, caressing every inch
Indulging my forbidden fruit until I reach a peak unheard of
We have something way beyond friendship or hugs,
something in between lust and love.

United by passions of our minds
Priceless like a Tupac rhyme.
In the past we were trapped in a world where words were unspoken
My soul is caged with rules unbroken
You lean on me, I lean on you
Doesn't it feel real when you're in the presence of truth?
You're a good friend; I would never leave you on the bench
Because the love I have for you is so immense.

Lifetime Friends

You are my best friend through thick and thin
I will always depend on my best friend.
You've always had my back
Never let me go off track, and I love you for that.

Mom and Dad, where do I start?
I can't give you the world, but here is my heart
All these years you held me up, and never gave up
You taught me to stay strong and to be tough
I owe you so much, you gave me life
Supported me whether I was wrong or right
When I made mistakes, you stayed there right by my side
My shoulder every time I cried.
My father, my hero, my strength.
My mother, my first love, my best friend.

You'll always be there when my friends are gone
You can live your whole life, but you only have one mom.
At times I was hard-headed and stubborn
And I know it seemed like I wasn't listening— but I was
And I am who I am now because of your love.
I'm drug and alcohol free
And I hope you are proud of me
Your baby girl, more precious than any pearl
You both kept me in hand when I cut loose
And because of that I will always love you.

I'd always have your back through all weathers
I couldn't have asked for any friends better
Not even if I wished
It's amazing how life hands us so many wonderful gifts
And the best gifts off them all is a lifetime of friendship with you.

You both opened my mind to love, trust— something I never knew .
Words can't express how deep my love for you goes
It's similar to how the Nile River flows
With every heartbeat it continues to expand
There is no dead end on how many times I will lend out my hand.

We Could Work

I think that we should be together, forever baby
Just give it a try
I see the way you look at me in my eyes, the heart never lies
It's been on my mind for quite some time
Didn't want to cross the line, but now I'm out of time.

Don't make her your wife, it will be a mistake
Together we'll be great
And I know you feel the same
Just sit and think
We could be a masterpiece
It could be you and me
I always had this dream
That my prince charming would sweep me off my feet
I feel that you are him, baby, come and get me.

I think you could be in my life forever
Remember when you said we belong together
I can't breathe without you next to me, it doesn't seem right
I can't live without you by my side
It's been a while since I've seen your smile— you always seem to be so hurt
If you were with me instead of her, I know we could work.

I can't help but think of the endless possibilities
If you were with me
Remember how it used to be
I messed up when I decided to leave
Now you have another woman
But I'm not bothered by it
Because I know you and I are a better fit
I just need you to get a grip and realize this
I want to stop you from making this huge mistake
But I won't, because I guess it's yours to make.

Open Your Heart

You underestimate yourself
You just need to believe
You let others bring you down
Maybe you are just too scared to succeed
Just take my hand and follow my lead
I know you want me, how can you not?
Everything will work out if you just follow your heart.

Maybe you like being mistreated
It's obvious, how can you not?
That's the only reason I believe that you play with fire in the dark.
With you I feel like I'm an angel sent to repair your lost soul
You can't fight the urge just let the holy take control.

It's easy to rebel and let evil in
But why forfeit when it was an easy win?
Only the weak accept defeat
The strong just keeps getting better
I stayed by your side through the troubled weather
I know that you need me, how can you not?
It'll be worth your while if you just open your heart.

Make Me Feel

Nothing can match the depths of the way I feel
A feeling so fairytale, but significantly so real
You have shown me things I was too stubborn to see
Taught me to cherish even the most microscopic things
Gave me a reason to breathe, ambition to believe
That true love was waiting for me.

Enriched with your lovely presence; You are a true blessing
You gave me insight, gave me a will to fight
When I thought I was all I needed, you appeared in my life
Ups turn down, but we never fall off
Embraced my strengths and weakness; my perfections and flaws
You make me feel tall, even when I am not at all.

You protect me in ways no one else has
You put my mind on the future and made me put back the past.
You make me feel happy, you make me feel sad
You make me cry, you make me laugh
You make me want, you make me give
You make me a better person, because of you I live.

I'm in love it's so crazy, I breathe you daily
Only you hit spots which make me quiver
In the summertime you make me shiver
You're the half of my whole, the mate to my soul
Without you I'm out of control, but with you all is possible
You are everything that I desire
There is no love any higher.

I've never been one to catch feelings,
Then it comes when I least expect it.
Our electric connection is so infectious.

Being in your presence is a present.
A love so strong, it breaks down my walls
Answering a call I didn't know was mine at all.
You came like a storm, but gentle and true,
Changing my world with everything you do.

You make me feel seen in a world that's so blind
Unraveling the chaos that lives in my mind.
With every word, you calm my fears
With every touch, you dry my tears.
You're my peace, my light, my gentle embrace
My heart feels at home in your sacred space.

Life would be pointless if a queen had no king
Where would I be if you weren't here with me?
Most of all you make me feel
Something I was incapable to do in the past
You and me, that's all we need
That's all we need to last.

Eternally

Loving you comes natural like night and day
Like the moon you are the light which guides my way
Like the sun, shielding my soul from this frigid world
No mountain too high or ocean to deep, I'll always be your girl.

I know you're the one, God sent me a sign
You're the cells to my brain—without you, there's no mind.
If loving you was a crime, consider me on death row
I'd do anything for you, except for let you go.

You are the reason I wake up to see another day
You leave me speechless
I can't put to words what my heart wants to say
I love your sexy brown eyes and soft luscious lips
With a smile so content.

I don't know how to act, but I am definitely in love
Because my heart melts from your touch and your hug
All my life I've waited to exhale, the wait is over
I want to be the mother of your children, your wife, your soldier.

What's Love?

Now out the blue you want to leave
I gave you two years of my life, faithfully
So, what's love?
Over and over it flowed from your tongue
I thought I couldn't breathe, it felt like I had no lungs
You would come in at all hours of the night
Love must be blind
You had me like Stevie Wonder, I could not see right.

Cold shoulders and shivering nights
While I stayed gripping the pillow tight
I needed you next to me, caressing me
Fist fights, you said you would never raise a hand
I tried to raise a boy to be a man, but you can't.

How long are you going to let our son see us unstable?
Alone, I had to put food on the table
We had mouths to feed
You were in the penitentiary, and you left me with your seed
I cried so many tears I could flood the earth
You never thought to put this woman first.

It's supposed to be 50/50 and I'm putting in 100%
I told you I forgave you, but I will never forget
When you crept with your baby mom and women at the bar
You lied to me, I found used Trojans in the car.

You once were my heart, my soul, my best friend
You contribute to 99% of my mistakes
No more lies for you to make
And no more abuse for me to take
I must be stupid to love you.

When our son was born, where were you?
When he died minutes later, where were you?
Take this ring, I'm through!

I can do bad by my damn self
You aren't halfway worth the pain I felt
It's over, you're no longer my man
You always wanted a hand
I gave you an arm and you took two legs
You tried to break me, you couldn't, and I still stand.

Prisoner's Song

Dear love, I stuck by your side through the good and bad stuff
Don't think that I'm going to leave now
when the going gets tough
You're my diamond in the rough; just keep your head up
I keep stacks on your commissary
I am holding it down, don't worry.

Depressed, your mom sends her best, although she is stressed
I'm making sure she gets her rest, and that she takes her meds
Just watch your back, don't get misled.
And don't stress about Arnez, he's dead
And dead men don't talk
We got the appeal, so soon you will walk
Your visitations, I'm there first thing
How can I forget about you baby?
I'm wearing your ring!

And your friends are foul, trying to get in
between my vertical smile
I can't give up on you now
Every bad boy needs a bad girl to hold him down
Yeah, baby girl has your smile, and wow, little man is walking now
They miss their dad
All cried out, I need you bad!

I hate to see my bird caged
I must escape just to stay sane.
But no pain, no gain
I love you— I know you feel the same
I hope you maintain
I know how prison makes a man change.

When you're locked up, your mind dies
This can't be our life
I won't stop until our hearts are healed
Hugs and kisses, signed and sealed.

Lover's Lane

Never hold on to someone that's not trying to be kept
Because I can do bad by my damn self
I'm leaving you, I'm through with it
I bring up the past because I still live through it
Karma is real, you sew what you reap
And you'll never find another woman quite like me.

You're playing games in this lover's lane
There are no sunny days, it seems like just rain
Is it love or hate when it's all pain?
Ladies, use your brain, or did he beat you insane?

You are always making excuses for him, saying phrases like:
"He only hit me because he loves me down"
"He only cheats when I'm not around"
"He'll never kiss her or go downtown"
"I'm cuter than her"
"He thinks about me when he's intimate with her"
Girl, how dumb does that sound?
And you fell for it like a clown.

You were on that no air mess and couldn't breathe
Constantly crying yourself to sleep, "Like damn, why did he leave?"
Asking yourself crazy things
Like, "What was it about me? Am I ugly?"
"Why don't he love me?"

Don't cry tears to flood the earth
Just learn to put yourself first
I know you never felt like this
You fell in love with a dog and you just got bit
He started out so sweet, but turned out so vicious.

They say you don't know what you got until it's gone
He'll think about that when he realizes he was wrong.

Disgusted

Quiet, you'll wake up the kid
I can't believe six years I put up with your mess
I'm through, of course I love you, but I'm sick of it
What does love have to do with this?
Apparently, nothing!

I'm tired of your fussing
We went from lusting to cussing
From breaking up to making love
With you— I'm disgusted!
You scarred my trusting
I needed a man, and that you were not.

When you were locked up, I put my jewelry up to post your bail
And now I'm like, "What the hell?"
I should have left your sorry tail to rot in jail
Oh, please don't flip it on me
I followed you and Jen to the Holiday Inn
And I know you been with Crystal
I got proof on my digital.

You had a winner
But you passed her up for a sideline nut
I'm strong, I'll move on
I will not break!
You wanted icing, so where's the cake?
Just cry me a river like Timberlake.

My Lord

He said let there be light, and it came on
My dad was at war in a fight, and he came home
That's why I believe, God's right here with me
No matter what you think, He is the reason I sing.

My Lord will always keep me safe
My Lord would never ever stray away
My Lord is here to stay
My Lord could never ever be replaced
My Lord is so great, He's so great.

You can't take Him from me
No one will ever love me like He does
I believe in my Lord
There's no one like my Lord
People ask me, how do I keep faith?
They ask me how I can trust someone I don't see
How the world is going crazy, yet I still believe.

It's because I feel Him inside me
The Lord He always guides me
Without Him there will be no me
That's how I can believe.

Why Do You Hurt Me?

We could have had it all
Two kids and a picket fence
Growing old together like the Jeffersons
We could have had it all
We could have been the real-life Huxtables
Baby, we could have been untouchable
We didn't make it this far for it all to end now
What happened to our vows?

Deception, lies, heartache is what happened
All of this when I finally thought I could trust
That's the difference between love and lust
I loved you and you betrayed me
You made those vows sacredly, and said we would always be.
One year and six months was our forever, apparently
Why do you continue to hurt me?

How could you go near her?
How could you jeopardize our life together?
For one night of pleasure
That is not love
Why even commit if you know you can't be faithful?
I thought we were unbreakable
What is it? Do you want to turn me hateful?

Do you enjoy seeing me hurt? Do you thrive off my heartache?
It really disappoints me because I thought we were in a good place
You want to make us work— but why would I stay?
You have broken me to the core
And I deserve so much more.

You keep lying, like you are trying, but you know you are not
And I keep crying, I can't deny it, these tears just won't stop
I try to play it cool when I notice you talking to other girls
You said you love me, boo
You said that I'm the one for you
You said I'm your whole world—But why do you hurt me?

Sibling Love

Through better or worse, Ranada, you were there first
Way before my birth, you had my back when I was hurt
Ernest, you protected me, and never neglected me
I know sometimes you may think I treat you wrong
But I trust it will only make you strong.

Chris, we connect on so many levels
You have a big heart and so spiritual
You are so kind, and you have so much ahead of you
I hope you succeed in everything that you do.

Alex, you give the best advice
Always spoke your mind though sometimes shy
You are beautiful, baby bro, you have so much potential
I just want to say thank you.

Five warriors, one fight was our fight
We had each other's back even if we disliked
Always had someone to talk to, I never was alone
Long distance, we still picked up a phone.

And I know I was a motor mouth
And I often loved to pout
Thanks for putting up with me
Thanks for everything
My best friends, you all keep me on my feet
You never steered me wrong
And that's why I wrote this poem.

One Kiss

All I need is one date, one night, and one kiss
If I had one wish, that would be it.
So, I met this woman about a year ago
I can't explain it completely, but we connected souls
A few weeks later I got her number
I really wanted to get to know her
But we were just friends, and she had a man
That kind of messed up my plans, I'm like 'Take me, leave him!"

I didn't think they would work
Because in her eyes I saw so much hurt
We started getting close, I texted her love notes
At first to me it was a joke, but my heart did not think so
Then she met another man, he was better for her.
She broke up with her boyfriend, and started talking to him
While me and her were still just friends
But I wanted in, give me a chance
Damn, she's a month pregnant... And thinks it's her ex man's kid
I didn't feel excellent, I wanted to pass out, I had cramps
Now I will never get a chance!

It's not like I was going to anyways
Neither one of us was gay
But I guess it was something I wanted to try
So, I guess that makes me bi
But everything feels alright when I glance in her eyes
And now she has a man again
Back to square one again
But there's no point, we are not meant to be
Because we both desired to be with Kings, and not Queens.

One Day You Will

You don't miss me now but one day you will
I'm the best thing since hot meals
You are just played like hot wheels
Because I'm a hot deal
We were friends for five years, now it all ends here.

You don't miss me now, but fact is
You had too much baggage
An ex still in your life, too many bad habits
I was devoured by a savage
But karma will soon ravage.

You don't miss me now, but I will not cry
You looked me right in the eyes and lied
I kept you out of jail, and in return you give me hell
Oh well, I must keep my guard up
I trusted for once and got stuck.

You don't miss me now, but that's okay
Sooner or later you will realize your mistakes
I'm the last of a dying breed
What other woman can compete?
You are not even worthy
You never did deserve me.

You miss me now, but you're out of luck
You're playing games, and you need to just grow up
You are no friend
You are just pretend.

Another Love Triangle

I never thought you would be the one to steal my heart
Here is the dilemma; here is what tears us apart
You have a girlfriend, and then there's me on the side
You say that you love me, you like her, but I know it's just lies
We both have feelings for each other so what's the problem then?

We can no longer be friends
It is too hard to when I am still in love with you
I try to distance myself, but I can still smell your scent on my clothes
I wish this excruciating pain would just disappear
I don't want to hurt, I don't want to cry— why are you even still here?
Losing our friendship is my worst fear, but I can't stay away,
and I can't stay near.

Why did we let this fling occur?
Do you think about me when you are screwing her?
Do you think about her when you are screwing me?
I can't even get a kiss, is it because you feel guilty?
I come up with the conclusion that you are just using me
Broken promises and lies, baby you are losing me
I can't understand, is it her or me?

Why did you say you love me?
What is so good about her?
What is it that she does that I can't do?
Because I am better than your girlfriend times two.

I hate the fact that I love you
Constantly crying at night thinking of you
Why are you trying to hold on to me?
Why when I call, and she is there you just let it ring?
That's not the way it used to be, do you even care for me?

Lately, you are never there for me like you should be
Am I just a backup plan in case she ever leaves?
Where do I stand?
Tell me please!

Your relationship is all lies
Six months of you cheating on her, that's a long time
You said our bond is closer, so let her go
I refuse to just wait around until you grow
I need to know, I don't want to feel this pain anymore.
I want all or nothing, or there's the door.

Can't Be Friends

We can't be friends
I just hate the thought of it
Imagining you with another female
That's the hardest
Another woman's lips on your lips
Another woman tasting your kiss
Another woman driving your stick
I just can't do this!

I'm thinking about how you ran out on me
Mother always told me
"If you buy him shoes then he'll walk right out on you"
And I'm living proof that is true
You left me in tears, crying myself to sleep
And now you want to be friends with me?

As if nothing ever happened between us
Just last week we were in deep love
Now look what you've done
There's no way in Hell I can just forget and move on
I can't fake it; it's too soon and too fast
I can't just pretend we had no past.

Worth It

For every break in my heart
I've learned a lesson
For every tear that I shed
I pray there's a blessing
So many mountains to cross
I hope I don't get lost
I'll just follow my heart
And pray it leads me home, back to you
For I would be the most blessed
I keep taking forward steps
But at times I feel that it is hopeless
It seems impossible to get back in your good graces
But it would be worth it.

Am I Really Sure?

Wanted to be forever, we said we'll always be together
But am I really sure?
Can I handle your outbursts, your being immature?
Are you really the one for me?
Are we really meant to be?
Am I really sure?

Soul so pure, heart so kind
But can I really, really love you for your mind?
So childlike, so childlike,
Am I really sure?
Mr. Right, Mr. Right,
Or do I need much more?

How come not a normal man
But acts like he's three
I just don't understand, or maybe it's just me
Maybe I'm being cursed from my mistakes in the past
Maybe karma's haunting me, left me with a man that's thrashed.

I don't want my kids growing up confused
I don't want my kids acting older than you do
My patience is wearing out, what should I do?
I'm in love with a little boy who is age twenty-two.

You give me pleasure, but cause me pain
Your childish ways, makes me ashamed
I wish I would have known you, before your mind was scattered
I know my positive influence would have very much mattered
I can't lie, you treat me so right
But please understand how I feel inside.

Yes, I know you had a rough life
Go ahead, spread your wings, I'll teach you how to fly
You can't have a future living in the past
I'll guide you the way, but first you need to let go of the bad.

I've outgrown the games, the laughs that don't last
I'm building a future while you're stuck in the past.
We're walking two roads that no longer align
I crave a partner, not someone to guide.
I love you, I do, but love isn't enough
I need a man who can stand up when life gets tough.

No Protection

So, you trust him with your life?
You trust that you are the only one he is with, right?
You're willing to put everything on the line for that man?
A man that has yet to put a ring on your hand.

So, you trust him that much?
With your most precious gift?
Jesus died so we could live
And you give your life to your man
Is that what you're saying?

You trust this man with your life?
You let him bareback
Just trusting that it's only you
But what if it isn't?
You put your life in this guy's hands
But what if he is going raw with other women?

How is he to protect you when he uses no protection?
And you just believe him, he just believes you
You're risking your lives daily
Trusting that the trust is mutual
Until you realize it's not
So, then you get tested
And discover you're infected
All because you trusted his protection.

Miles Apart

When we first met, I knew we would forever connect
Which is why I could not bear to let you go?
Although, we were on different levels at the beginning
I wanted something serious, but you weren't willing
It was wonderful just us chilling.

Then you gave in, and became my man
Being with you is so amazing.
I tried to pretend I wasn't falling, but I fell hard
You filled the hole in my heart, and it's no longer scarred.
With every touch, every word, you healed the past
Turning pain into love, making something that lasts.

I see through you, I know you care more than you say
No need to fear love, just let me lead the way
I'm not like other women, I won't leave you astray
And you'll always have a place in my heart, even miles away.

It's difficult seeing my bird in a cage
Baby, keep your head up, it will all be okay.
We will get through this phase
Distance may test us, but love still remains.

In Memory

No tissue is immense enough to hold these tears that I cry
For you are the reason I get up in the morning to see another day
I know you're protecting us when we are asleep at night
God must have been lonely without you
Because he took his angel back upstairs
And took you home to be with Cousin Jay
I miss going home to Indianapolis
Where Aunt Sandra took turns braiding our hair
The nonstop laughter we shared
Remember little Derrick's basketball game? —We giggled with tears
You are the sweetest and kindest person I've ever known
No matter who was at fault you took anyone in your home
You always forgave and forgot
I wish one day I could be like you
You had a lovely smile that shone rainbows through a heated room.
Your presence was uplifting
You loved all who came in contact
You are truly the world's gift
I love you Aunt Deborah
In Heaven we shall meet again.

Left for Dead

He said he'd always be there and he'd always would care
He said I meant the world to him and without me there's no him
But why does he tell me lies? Why does he waste my time?
Just tell me the reason why, and look me in my eyes
He took my innocence, he took my youth
So now he owes me the truth.

I fell in love with a monster, with a face of an angel
I didn't know he was a monster, until he put me through Hell
He got me crying and crying, feeling like I'm dying
Why did he do this to me?
I know I should leave
I should go and pawn this ring
Because he got the best of me.

What's all the money in the world if you don't have a soul?
Got diamonds and pearls but your heart is so cold
He treated me so bad and took everything I had
He even took my smile and then my laugh
Then he left me for dead.

This will be your last time hurting me like you do
This will be your last time because I'm through with you
No more playing and no more games
I can see the real you, you are never changing
I don't know what I'm doing, I feel so confused
I must leave, I must find me
I must move on, and I must be strong.

The last straw was when you put your hands on me
I must get back my dignity.

I was blind but now I see
I don't care about your money.

I trusted a monster in an angel disguise
His intent was dishonor and he had hate in his eyes
Now in my adult life still feeling so deprived
Because he robbed me of my youth
And now I feel of no good use.

Something New

Our future's in danger because I am lying next to a stranger
You're not the one I fell in love with
The man I met no longer exist
You're just an eggshell of yourself
And I'm screaming out for help
S.O.S. someone save me
Take away this man and bring back my baby
It seems you like who you are, but I love who you were
We're growing apart, but I really want to make it work.

From death until we part and through old age
Those are the vows we made
You will always have my heart, but now it doesn't feel the same
Because we're both going through change
I really love you, and I know you love me too
We really need to think this through, I don't want to start new
I don't want to lose you, what are we going to do?

You're changing, I'm changing, we're changing up
I gave you all my time and gave you all my love
But it doesn't seem to be enough
I gave you my heart, I gave you all my trust
But I'm falling out of love
We must spark this flame and make our love reign again
We must remember why we fell in love in the first place
We must make it right.

Are we going to make it work, put us first,
And fall in love with the new?
Or are we going to give up, throw away our love,
And move on to something new?
Tell me—what are we going to do?

Forever Love

I need a forever kind of love
That's what I'm accustomed to
My parents are happily married
They've been together forever
My grandparents did the same
So when I look for love, it has to last for an eternity
And that will never change.

I need someone that will love me endlessly and unconditionally
It seems this new generation only love under conditions
So if the slightest thing goes wrong
Then their relationship is out of commission
That's why the divorce rates are ridiculously high
I'm not saying every couple who stays together is perfect
But when you know what you have, and it's worth it,
Then you actually try!
Some people are too lazy to put the work in
That's when one person feels unappreciated and overwhelmed
Then the problems begin to seep in
If you both don't pull your weight, then you won't win.

No obstacles can come in between real love
Because whatever comes up against us will tumble
United, we're like vibranium, and no boulders can make us crumble
I need an old fashioned man whose honest and loyal
A king to make me his queen, we will treat each other royal.
I want that chemistry that no other person can match
My dream man will always make me laugh
I want someone I can have fun with
But also holds everything down like a real man should
A protector, a provider, doing everything in his power that he could
I need someone who matches my heart.

Growing old together, and keeping the vow—
'until death do us part.'

I need a love that transcends time
A bond so pure, so deeply divine.
Through every trial, we'll only grow fonder
Like rivers to oceans, our love will flow yonder.
Through seasons of joy and storms of despair,
We'll conquer it all with a love so rare.
Building a legacy, hand in hand,
Writing our story in the sacred sand.

Wide Awake

I'm wide awake to your BS
Yes, I must confess
I was blinded by the penis
But now I must leave— we're through!
Your mask fell off, I can now see the real you.

I was at home alone
While you were gone
Doing whatever you pleased
Then I began to think
I've been lying next to a stranger for years
No ring on my finger, so why am I still here?

I've been in denial as if we were in sequence
But now I know we were just convenient
Communication and trust we lacked
Time to get my self-respect back.

I'm not taking any more of your sorry apologies
Go ahead let your actions speak
I thought I would get pleasure from revenge
Just knowing I put you through the same pain
But karma won't be looking for my name.

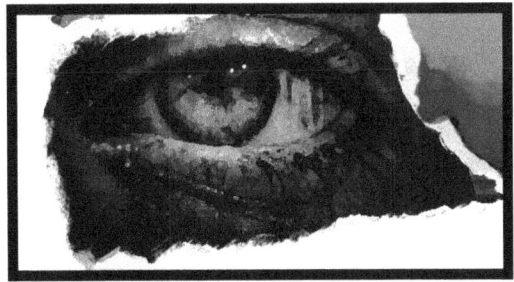

Leap Love

We got married in a leap year on Feb 29th
Maybe that was the sign
That our love wouldn't last forever
Maybe we just weren't meant to be together
Maybe we weren't the right fit
We were in each other's lives for a purpose
But maybe it was not our time
Maybe you were never mine
We chose a day that constantly fades
It is skipped over for three years, then reappears.
Maybe that's why it wasn't our fate.

Because like our anniversary date, our *love* disappeared.
So I guess
        we had
                leap love.

Queen

Her resilience stands tall, unmatched,
Her focus sharp, her vision intact.
She's navigated storms with precision and grace,
Unshaken by critics who can't take her place.

Through seasons of envy, through shifting tides,
She stayed grounded, her strength her guide.
Newcomers crumble, not built for this climb,
But she reigns eternal, defying time.

Queen of Rap—no one compares,
Across all eras, she remains top tier.
She's reshaped the game, her influence vast,
A legacy infinite, forever to last.

No award or accolade will ever measure her impact,
She's unstoppable, she's proven to be the best.
She shattered records, inspired a wave,
Now others can flourish on the path she paved.

The industry's treatment is unjust, unfair,
But God's got her; He's always there.
Karma spins back, the truth prevails,
The Queen's resilience never fails.

From Queens she rose, the world in awe,
Breaking the mold, rewriting the law.
Her heart in her art, her spot cemented,
Her impact is global, her power relentless.

When she speaks, her words ring true,
Her artistry rare, her caliber few.

So here's to the Queen, forever our muse,
Giving us hope when there's nothing to lose.

The Queen called my rap perfect—her words a crown,
A moment so surreal, I'll never come down.
She taught me to rise above, to fight, to be,
A reflection of her artistry.

PART 2:
CASUALTIES OF LIFE

So Sick

There are tags on your toes with a price for your soul
Because nothing in this life is free
You can run but you can't hide
Just open your eyes
Because the devil never falls asleep.

Where I'm from, you either get it or get lost
Or like waves in the ocean you will get tossed
Some sell their souls at all cost just to floss
But I don't need to be false to prove I'm a Boss.

My dignity will never let that be me
No lie, the truth shall set you free
I done seen it all, and done it all; So, you can't make me fall
I am Syleena Johnson tall, because I'm still standing like a stone wall.

I rang the liberty bell, for those that crumbled and fell
To say I won't excel, is like saying that it's ice cold in Hell
We must think deep like a well, because society is crazy
It's a dog eat dog world, and nobody is in safety.

And they ask me, why I don't have any babies?
Raise a child in these days? You must be crazy
One day maybe
God is the truth, I'm living proof
I could have died in that accident
But He gave me a second chance.

I am so sick of the raindrops
Please tell me when the pain stops; I feel bank robbed
All these haters trying to take mine
But they get no dime
Out of sight, out of mind
Just let me live my life.

Dark Clouds

Dark clouds are all over me
They say I am Hell bound noticeably
So, I'm not trying to die
Just look into my eyes
What do you see?
There's a soul of a sinner
I survived through the blizzards
So my heart is a winner.

What happened to my life?
Well, I'm not living swell
Anger aggressive female that is always flirting with jail
I can't seem to find a decent male
I feel cursed because when it snows it hails.

We call this life, why?
Most of us just living to die
Heartless, I rather kill than cry
Maybe that's why, this world is not right
Your heart is empty, very light
Christ, what's missing?
Maybe because you never lived your life Christian.

This goes to those that are innocent
But are still about to get sentenced
This is dedicated to those domestic violence victims
Or those that are cancer stricken
Keep your head afloat
Never let them sell you short
God is the truth, I'm living proof
I could have died in that ditch
But He let me live!

Missing Cycle

We've been together, now, over eight years
Now what gives you the right to just disappear?
Two months in withdrawal, come back to me
I can't face the fact of what I am about to be
This position right now just can't be me
I'm going to college and healthy, I am still a teen
What will the family think?

My mom will disown me
Ever since Eve did the forbidden
You have been a curse to all women.
I never wanted to see blood so much
Even if it's just a touch
I'm begging in my time of need
Please lady P, come back to me!

I don't even want to think
I must take a test, I need to see
What if the stick turns pink?
This is surreal, I can't be
This just isn't my life, this isn't me
I'm in disbelief!

I just know I'll be fine
It's taking too long, look at the time
Damn, is that really two lines?
I took the test already two times!
I can't believe it!
These tests are wrong, I won't conceive it.

Unborn

Another month past, I'm still in withdrawal
Lonely, confused, scared, I must let you go
Even though it hurts this part of me must die
I just got accepted into Harvard, I must live my life
I make good grades, but bad choices
It comes down to what I believe is more important
God, are you there? Please forgive me
I know it is murder, but the decision is not easy.

I'll be all by myself, no help
Broke, with no wealth
Struggling, that's not what I am about
Maybe when I am married, with a dog and a house
I can't imagine me homemaking
Really, basically I don't have the patience
It wasn't planned it was a mistake
I didn't think one night would determine my fate
I can no longer hide
It's time to decide
Do I want a life with freedom?
Or a life with pride?

{Fast-forward five years}
Dear baby,
You would have been four years old today
I was just a kid, so immature
I know I may seem selfish
And you're looking down on me from Heaven
I think about you every day
I have my degree
But I feel empty without you here with me
I can't believe I made such a huge mistake
I could have at least fought
I guess I was too concerned with what others thought.

Words Hurt Too

This piece is a metaphorical reflection, not a literal account of self-harm or violence.

Just words, just words, but are they just words?
You say they are just words, so they shouldn't hurt
But tell that to the kid that is at his worst
Blade to their wrist because of this
Contemplating ending it all— his life, that is!
So, are they just words?

When lives are lost because of what's heard
And kids are shooting up schools
Because they feel they have nothing to lose
So, are they just words?

When words spark pain that turns into hate
And then it fuels into rage
Feeling distraught
Feeling less than equal in heart
Sticks and stones do break bones
But words are how it all starts!
They are not just words!

No Clue

I must stand tall and keep my head up,
I know life isn't promised and it will gets tough.
We can't keep pointing fingers in blame
The only way forward, the only real change,
Is to start with the man in the mirror
That's the only way to make this clearer.

You must fight through the rain
It's the only way to push through pain.

You have no clue why I hide my tears in a disguise,
Why I wake up in cold sweats in the middle of the night
Trapped in my fears, lost in my cries, drowning inside.
Most think I'm tough as nails, but I'm soft as cloth
Travel my thoughts, and you're bound to get lost.

We're not made of glass, but everybody breaks.
We all fall like leaves,
but it's up to us—
do we rise again, or just get raked?

Blind Society

If I were blind, I wouldn't see crime—
racism, rape, or filth-stained grime.
I wouldn't see killers taking lives,
Or children preyed on before their time.

Step inside my mind, let's take a ride
I wonder if losing sight would leave me deprived?
The things I see in this frigid world make me cry.
I wonder what life looks like through Stevie Wonder's eyes
Where there's no sight of homicide or suicide
No haunting guilt that lingers inside,
From staring helpless in a loved one's hopeless eyes.

I can't bear the trauma society made me endure,
My lenses are damaged, my vision's impure.
Sometimes I wish I didn't see the world this way,
or that others could see through my view for a day.

I'm tired of saying goodbye to those who fall victim simply for living life
But if I were blind, would it ease my pain?
Or would I still hear the echoes of suffering remain?
A haunting sound that drives me insane.

It would be just my fate
I would still taste the bitterness your hatred creates
I would still smell the stench of death in the air.
I would still feel the tears of a victim's heir,
drenched in sorrow, heavy with despair.

So maybe I'd be better off senseless,
Numb to a world that's cold and relentless.

Woman of God

Beautiful, Strong and Educated, describes me completely
Head up and standing tall, that's the woman in me
You can try to shake me, try to break me, but you won't succeed
For I am a child of God and this is a woman you see.

Independent, Passionate, Proud
I don't need to brag or scream aloud
My presence can be easily found in massive crowds
It's not my shape or beauty that lures me out
But the grace within my smile
Because I'm a shining star from miles
And that's what being a woman is all about.

You can try to tear me down with your jagged tongue
But God built me with power and confidence— so I already won!
Faithful, Classy, Holy, is what describes me the best
I possess strength within because I learned from the best
A woman is a mother providing for her nest
Giving her all but never showing that she's stressed.

A woman is a sister with my secrets concealed
When the whole world is against me, she'll be there for me still
A woman is what I am
A Leader, Believer, Goal Achiever
Never backing down, no matter who deceives her
Always a shoulder to lean on when others need her
I look in the mirror with a smile
Because I'm a woman of God and proud.

Whole Again

I will find a way to get through this pain
Because I'm trying to feel whole again
Life has got me down, and it's hard for me to smile.
This is for those with hopes and dreams
Don't let doubters get you down on your knees
It's been a long time coming
But I'm not stopping for nothing!

Just don't try to push me when I'm on the edge
You can't keep a good woman down, that's what mama said.

I'm in a room full of people, but why do I feel so alone?
Like a prisoner caged in my own home
Has anyone asked why I cry?
Has anyone looked in my eyes?
Has anyone taken the time to realize that I'm dying inside?

If you could only feel how I felt
These are the cards that were dealt
But I can't keep living blind
Now my eyes are open wide
I just must live my life right.

There are so many hardships ahead
At times I'm feeling better off dead
I'm just lost in this quest
My soul is so full of pain
When will I feel whole again?

There is so much we face in this game of life
It could all be gone at the roll of a dice
We are not promised to live, we are on borrowed time
And it could all end at the drop of a dime.
Hopefully, by then, I will be whole again.

Road to Riches

Mama said to never settle for less
While I'm on this road to riches I'm steering my best
I'm never taking a left
You all can take that exit
But I'm going to ride the Lexus until the wheels are naked
That's my game plan
This is for the man that will never take a stand
Or the woman dealt a crappy hand
With dreams buried by a cruel circumstance
This is for the Preciouses that never stood a chance
Or those ridiculed by prejudice, because the color of their skin
I am living proof from rags to riches
I didn't have a pot to piss in
But I knew success was the mission
So, I kept my vision
I bear witness, from the start to the finish.

But, what about those who had it worst?
Like the kids who are cursed before birth
It's kind of hard for them to cope with life
When their mom is doped up, right?
Picture yourself in her shoes
Picture your uncle on top of you
What is a twelve-year-old to do?
She turns twenty-two with the same issues
It's the circle of life
We must break the mold and fight
Together we must unite
Because we are all the same color when you cut off the lights.

Adults get out your bible
We must change this vicious cycle
It starts with the parents first
You can't raise them right if you don't know your own worth.

Self-Esteem

You can't let life pass you by
Before you act out, you must think twice
Everything can all be gone in the blink of an eye
That's why we keep a smile through hard times.

This is for those who feel that they are living for nothing
I can't relate because I was always told I was something
I knew I was great before my creation
But some will never know how awesome they are
So I do this for those who were never told, "You are somebody"
Even though you were often told, "You are nobody!"

Keep the hope because it floats
You can never let them see you fold
Because they'll try to sell you short
On this road to the gold, some will sell their soul
I'm living for those who got TKO'd
But still rose!

Heaven only knows
This is the path you chose
I was often told to give them enough rope
Then they would hang themselves
He put his hands on you girl, and you blame yourself?
High self-esteem is wealth
Gain some confidence, that's the key to good mental health.

You're more precious than any jewel
You'll realize how easy life can be when you use your brain as a tool
And stop letting these creeps use you
Soon will be the time
You'll realize you're a gold mine.

I see your pain through your frown
Your light has been dimmed for a while
But now it's time for you to shine and smile
I see you looking at the mirror disgusted with your flaws
Making mountains out of moles, when there's nothing there at all
I wish you could see yourself like I see you
You're amazing, nothing short of beautiful!

You're despising yourself for what only you see as wrong
Ironic, because others envy you, as you've been flawless all along
Baby girl, you don't know how much you're worth
Until you learn to love yourself first.

Kids Raising Kids

Asking myself how bizarre I sound
To tell a nine-year-old to be strong and to be tough.
I mean she's just a kid, this must be rough
Her mommy acting her age, while she is burdened with adult stuff
As if that's not enough
She's the oldest of five girls so she is forced to grow up
Now she is constantly crying and crying, thinking it's all her fault
And her mom is just drowning in a bottle of Hennessey, so lost.

She's walking into danger, cheerful as can be
Because she doesn't realize her worst enemy is mommy.

I see the tears of despair
Mothers are supposed to give unconditional love
But this mom's actions say she don't care
Her family is trying to lend a hand for the children's sake
But she refused to reach— or even stand on her own two feet
Either you swim or sink, and life has her beat
She is twenty-six, but she looks forty-three.

So, when will this all end?
When you're dead and kids are orphans?

Confusion

Confusion is just a state of mind
We often fall—lost and blind.
Yet, in due time, it clears away,
revealing light beyond the gray.

You can often see pain hiding in blissful eyes
And if you listen harder, you'll hear sullen cries.
This is just the tale of my life
I'm just making sure you're alright.

I've been there before
Honestly, I'm not sure if I'm moving backwards or forward.
I thought I knew what life held, but now I'm clueless
And the mistakes we make often seem foolish.
But the sky is the limit, so we must seize each day.
Never give up, you must have faith.

At War

Kids are being sent to fight their parents' war
Picking up ammunition, but don't know what they're blasting it for.
Born into families where crime is tradition
Taught that cutting corners is the key to winning.
These kids aren't seeking a suicide mission
Just trying to survive, despite opposition.
Raised to be disrespectful and vicious
It's tragic they're manipulated, denied their innocence.
Parents should aspire for their kids to be better than them
Teaching them morals and values that will settle in.
Death is not what they are asking for.
The devil will answer if you keep beating on his door.
When it rains, it pours—
Parents need to be the shelter, not the storm.

In this game of life what's your score?
Seems like we are either rich still hustling—
or we are hustling poor.
I'm considered hopeless
A soldier, but not fallen, so I'm focused
The devil tried to intervene
He thought he had the best of me
But I'm still standing on my two feet
He tried to stop me, but I refused defeat
I'm going to conquer this world, just watch me.

I got to be all that I can be
Sometimes I feel like someone is watching me
Maybe it's my paranoia
I can't even trust my own shadow
I am afraid to look over my own shoulders.

Chasing Rainbows

I'm tired of chasing rainbows
That leads to no pot of gold
I tried the fork in the road
But just keep going in circles.

I always get the short stick
Instead of tricks we get tricked
When it rains it pours
But we must get through the storms.

I'm tired of giving my heart
Just to keep getting it torn apart
I'm tired of living a lie
So tired of these dark days and cold nights.

I've eaten life's forbidden fruits
So now it's time to face the truth
Society feeds off other's pain
And that is something that will never change.

My Psyche

Step into my life, my psyche
A world where the sun doesn't shine
Friends backstab just to get what is mine
This is my race against time
Existence for billions of years, yet the world is still blind.

A society where our youth fall victim to homicide
Suicide resides, but only the strong survive.
Your blood will betray, it will connive
Daily we are crossing this thin red line.
Envy, lust, jealousy, hate
These are the four devils of rage.

It's sad how infants are born with an incurable disease,
It's death before destiny breathes.
Isolated teens are unloading in schools,
Lost souls are drowning in their own blood pools.
We don't need any more drama
This is hell's kitchen—Satan's sauna.

In the trials and tribulations we survive,
Our conscience is constantly in good vs. evil fights.
And we are supposed to be sisters and brothers,
Yet we turn so quick to kill each other.
Yeah, many thought of it— we're human
But don't be stupid— don't do it!

It's less angels in a world of fate
Than devils in this world of hate.
So many scared to be chickens, but you are what you eat
This my broken silence and these wounds cut deep.

We're gagging on our own tears
We're just shadows of our own fears.

In this chaos, I search for the guiding light,
A beacon of hope in the endless night.
Though demons may whisper, I won't give in
My soul's battle is where healing begins.
The scars I carry tell stories untold,
Of a heart that's bruised but never cold.

And through God, all is possible, I'll rise,
Finding strength beyond what meets the eyes.
And through God, all is possible, I'll find,
Peace to heal the chaos in my mind.

Mother Nature

I watched them breathe life in and out of you daily
Pollution to your lungs, I watched them massacre your babies
We make it hard for you not to choke
Never dealt the hand, but I victimized secondhand smoke.

They spray your walls with poisonous substances
Suffocated your circuits
They are slowly draining your life support
They throw dirt on your feet, trash in your face
Mother, what kind of daughter dwells in your pain?

I've engraved writing in my siblings
What a harsh kind of living.
They burn iron, gases and coals into your heart
And then castrate your children.

For thirty-three years I have watched you die
Gave them the knife as they took your life
World, if you die on me, I know I'm to blame
For thirty-three years I watched them pollute your brain.

I watched your gates unfold, felt the chills of your cold
Ignored your violent storms, rain and fist of hail
Watched as your streets were flooded with shells
Ignored the cries of your winds
I want to tell you I'm sorry, but I don't know where to begin.

Awaiting Death or Prison

I'm trapped and it feels like hell
When you living life in J-Ville
A city with three options
Drugs, fast food, or armed forces
Limited opportunities limit your choices
Ostracized by the dominant portion
There's high rates of abortions
Teen pregnancies— they don't think
Lovers passing on STD's.

A city where friends are enemies
My friends are plotting for my man's meat
They say united we stand and divided we fall
But alone is when I feel I stand tall
I learned not to chase waterfalls, you will only drown in the long run
We're doomed for a place more scorching than the sun.

Your life is on the line— something like the movie *Phone Booth*
It's an eye for an eye and a tooth for a tooth
Revenge is sweet
But killing them with kindness is the sweetest defeat
It seems life is living us, but that's not my vision for me
Most people live awaiting death or prison
As if there's no real option to succeed
I'm a leader and I will never follow
So many individuals too bitter
I guess pride is just too hard to swallow.

You can't take me alive
Death has crossed my path twice— but I still survived
We are all to blame, it's a two-way street
What you sew you reap
I got a mind nobody can retrieve
People listen, understand, but just don't receive.

Fast Lane

I'm thinking, was taking that man's life really worth it?
Is judgement by execution the verdict?
Didn't he deserve to die?
He killed my cousin, so I did right, right?
I got tons of hatchets hanging over the head
You weren't the one at the funeral watching my aunt's tears shed
You weren't the one watching your closest get placed in the ground
I grabbed the weight of justice and silence was the last sound.

So how could you judge me?
What proves me guilty?
You never been where I been
I'm tired of the innocent getting thrown in the pen
Society is bleeding from affliction
World bound for flames — the Bible's prediction.

We need a resolution, world filled with overcrowded destitution
We're dying slowly from pollution, young girls trapped into prostitution
Children going to school with hate in their eyes
Little boys fall victim, shaped by the crimes.
This world will never change,
if we keep looking elsewhere to point the blame
Everything is just moving in the fast lane.

I'm walking through the fire, but I won't burn away,
They feed off my struggle, yet my soul won't decay.
The world is stained with grief, with pain, with poverty,
Head high because brighter days follow me.
Still, I dream of equality,
And unity could mend the wounds we carry as a society.
My strength is proof that they could never break me,
So, your last concern should be what I did to the enemy.

If I struck back at a murderer,
Then I saved the world from a predator,
Whose next stop could have been any of your daughters.
I'm furious that my cousin lost his life,
So I don't regret a thing from that night…

But the good in me won't let that transpire,
I woke up from my dream and realized I must rise higher.
I can't let evil win and drag me down,
I miss my cousin, but he wouldn't want me to drown.

I can't take a life for a life, I am not God,
Karma will spin back to the suspect twice as hard.
For I know the truth always finds its way,
And justice comes, if not now, then someday.

Revenge is a poison that corrodes the soul,
Forgiveness and patience make a spirit whole.
I carry his memory, I carry his name,
His light keeps me steady when I'm facing the pain.

A fictional reflection, not an endorsement of violence or revenge. It uses storytelling to convey pain and struggle, not literal events.

Why Forsaken Me?

Why forsaken me? I learned my lesson
I tried a confession, but I just wasted my time
Where I'm from it rains; the sun never shines
I'm not trying to be another statistic:
Wild Black child, three kids, and baby father missing.

I wish I can turn back the hands of time
Before I dealt with peer pressure and learned how to handle a nine
"Smoke this," "Drink this,"— it has to stop
Aunt died from cancer, and all I could do was sit back and watch
It's devastating
I would have done anything for her to make it.

And my grandma just passed away so it's hard for me to laugh
Wish I can turn the hands of time back
But she's safer in God's path
Than this world full of combat
Life's nothing but a game of chess
And we're just pawns awaiting death.

So many pregnant teens, 5 months and still denying
And weeping mothers on their knees crying
I got rage, but I would never act on it
Instead I substitute guns for paper and use ink as bullets
We need more Harriet Tubmans and Martin Luther Kings
That way we can balance out the foolish
Life is nothing but a maze and we are guinea pigs
We must make some changes in this world—
because I just don't get it.

Battlefield

This life is a battlefield
It can get so real, when you're alone with no shield
Some may feel like Samuel L. Jackson in *A Time to Kill*
When you're cornered but unbroken, with Magnolia's steel
You're just living for the thrill
While some are living for a meal
Your fate is signed and sealed
So, do as you will.

I must breakaway
I must get out of my own way
We must stop pointing the blame
And get in our own lanes
I learned on my own to crawl
United we stand, divided we fall
But alone I stand tall.

I will never chase waterfalls
You will just eventually drown
It's a dog eat dog world, can't let life get you down
I stay focused, never counting sheep
Karma's on your back so you sew what you reap
Mama always told me to practice what you preach
So, I won't stop until the world's under my feet.

This battlefield is life itself — the fight to endure, not a literal war.

Hold On

Meet Chris, a street pharmacist, he was my best friend
Outside looking in, just trying to fit in
A little man, unprepared for a grown man's game
On the street corners dealing the cocaine
Until the car crept up and pumped lead through his brain
Fourteen years old, what a shame
But it wasn't his time
In Junior High and paralyzed at the spine.

He thought he knew secrets to life, but had no knowledge
Always thought he'd go off and make it big in college
He wasn't ready for the world, he just followed
Now he's on life support— hollow
So, his life is on hold, his mama crying out "No!"
"Why my baby? He's only fourteen years old"
So young, so immature
He has so much ahead to live for!

She can't let him go, imagine her sorrow
A pill too hard to swallow
Something must give
She's watching her youngest kid fight to live
As she's just fighting her tears.

This can't be life at all
Five feet trying to walk tall
But there must be hope
She's just trying to stay afloat
Nowhere to go, forty-four-year-old and suicidal
She has nothing to live for, her self-esteem is so low
One son on his death bed and the other son on death row.

She feels so alone—
Crying in the house, but she can't call it a home
Depressed, so she turns to her role model
Nothing but a bag of trees and a brown bottle.

But in the darkness, a small voice speaks
A whisper of strength for the days that seem bleak.
Through the pain and the trials, she starts to pray
Hoping for light to break through the gray.
She clings to faith, though her world's torn apart
Fighting for her family with all of her heart.

She remembers the words her mother once said,
"Even in storms, you must lift your head."
With trembling hands, she opens a book,
The Bible, her refuge, gives her hope another look.
"For I know the plans I have for you," it reads
A promise of healing, a planting of seeds.
Though her world feels shattered, her spirit must mend,
Believing this brokenness isn't the end.

Sweet Talker

He was a sweet talker, and a ladies man
Pretty boy player who went from pants to pants
Golden skin tone and corn rows in his head
Basketball captain, a very popular kid
He thought the world was to bow to his feet
Reality, he's twenty years old with H.I.V.

He felt ashamed, with pleasure comes pain
He had plans for his life
To finish college, then pro-ball, kids and a wife
Now it's hard to sleep at night
Day to day there's a fight for his life
He had everyone eating from the palm of his hands
Class king, but now has no friends.

It's crazy how things change when water runs dry
It's insane how ups turn down at the blink of an eye
Have you ever seen a grown man cry?
Moved too fast, now he paid that price
Only wish is to wake up from this dream
But reality is he's twenty years old with H.I.V.

Yet, through the pain, he finds his way
Learning to cherish each new day.
Not just a past, but a future to see
A chance to live, to love, to be free.

No longer bound by shame or fear
Strength in his heart, purpose is clear.
Life goes on—though not as planned
He stands tall, a stronger man.

Different Visions

I wonder if my parents split up, how would I end up?
Would I be a run-away? Or a slut? Would I be fast in the butt?
Will I still be determined and content with learning?
Or would I be trouble, on the hustle just popping muscle?

Kim's parents divorced, and now she is all buck wild
She is running from the law now, at age fifteen with child
But Laura's parents split, now she is enrolled in pre-medicine
She is twenty-two with no kids, and her own place to live
What's the difference?
What has changed? What is missing?
We all grew up together in the suburbs with the same way of living
We had similar situations but just different visions
I tried to tell Kim, but she didn't listen.

Now five years later, same girl, but so lost in this world
She was molested as a child, now she is still buck wild
Always drunk in the club, showing every man love
Now she hates herself
Always spending her money on liquor, so she has no wealth
Three kids, and she is a high school drop out
She works at Burger King, but she always calls out
She doesn't know what she wants out of life
Low self-esteem, but the girl looks so fine.

She can feel death calling, twenty-year-old alcoholic
She got married so young, but now she is separated
Abusive relationships are all that she faces
Her lights are cut off constantly
The kids are freezing cold, because there is no heat
She has some twisted priorities.

Her family extended their hands, but she said "Let me be"
Now it's too late, she O.D.'s.

It's sad that she was lost, and had no clue what life was about
And I feel bad because I knew her
I tried to school her and help her out
So common, it's scary how the circle of life goes
But we must be smart and break this cycle.

The Heat of the Night

It's Hell in this world, but I must get by
It's Hell in this world, but I must survive
It's Hell in this world, but I must get through
I must pay my dues, I must make moves.

Love hurts, so I hurt love
I keep my friends close, and enemies even closer
I am a Holy Ghost soldier
And I will not get toasted up over you vultures
Society is testing our race, like we're guinea pigs in a maze
And they blame it on rappers by pointing fingers our way
Saying the things that they say give kids criminal ways
But they have nothing to say when rock stars do the same
As the world keeps turning, the truth gets ignored
The rich stack their wealth while the poor stay worn.

I want to leave, but how can I fly with broken wings?
Why does the devil keep on provoking me?
I feel blessed in this life but cursed at the same time
Even now, we still see hate crimes.
Kids can't add but they can take away lives
I saw on the news a little girl was pregnant at age nine
This just isn't right
Teens know how to fight, but they can't read and write
We are living the days of our lives in the heat of the night.

Fighter

Eight pounds, fourteen ounces—a baby girl
It's kind of impossible how I came into this world
I am blessed, I can't ignore that
The umbilical cord was wrapped around my neck
So even in the womb, I was fighting for breath
Went blow for blow with death and I came out unscathed.

One year old with meningitis
But this girl was a fighter
Now thirty-six years later this woman is a survivor
But history repeats itself
Choking, gasping for breaths
Can you hear me Lord? I need your help.

Life is what you make it
You can sit back waiting
But I'm going to take it
The sky is the limit
A fighter is in it
Never give up whether shy or timid.

You can never judge a book by its cover
And you can't judge someone's will by their skin color
Friends backstab just to get my ends
Blood is thicker than water— but even kin is thin
Snakes are on my lawn, and the hating is blatant
Lord please forgive them, although they side with Satan.

It's Too Late

Written in the 90s when I was around 12, this poem reflects my young heart processing loss and the impact of A.I.D.S. during that time.

You used to be the concerned one,
The first to have fun.
You used to stay out all night,
Now staying out past six is a fight.

You used to worry about me
Because I was the youngest of us two,
But now I worry about you.

You used to be so healthy,
Until A.I.D.S. killed you.

Haters

I'm so high above the sky
Who is touching me now?
And I can't fall just fly
It's a long way down
I must be V.I.P.
As much as y'all discuss me
Ooh, y'all disgust me
Always wishing y'all was me.

Once you succeed
Then there they'll be
Nit-picking the small things
Like your clothes and your feet
Praying that you fall defeat
But you'll never see me weak
Truth is, you hate me
Because you're not me.

Really, it's sad
What you could have
If you applied half of that energy on yourself instead of me
Talking about my success isn't going to last
Why are you so mad?
Is it because I'm on top getting everything you're not?

When you are on the rise like escalators
It's only fit to expect the haters
Shout out to those who hated
Because of you I made it
You thought I'd fold and take it
Nope, it just made me the greatest.

Insecurities

Having a baby won't keep these men
I try to tell that to so many women
They keep trying to trap him to stay
But if he didn't love you in the first place
Then that won't change
Instead you would take a risk
By bringing a child into this world without stability
All because of your insecurities.

Worth More

Success must be measured in cups
Because the morals of some of these young ladies are messed up
You went from honor roll to most honored hoe
And I'm not judging you, though
I'm just trying to help you grow
To do something more than porn videos
And sliding down a dirty pole.

Young girls, we deserve more
We are worth more
Than one-night stands and cold sores
Or Plan Bs and being called whores.

You'd rather settle for a man who is on the corner selling rocks
And turn down a man with a 9-5, because he's not that hot
Or reject a man with a degree, claiming he has no swag
Then wonder why your kids have no dad,
Because your man is incarcerated, his choices were bad.
Why would you rather be with a dude who puts his hands on you?
I've never walked in those shoes
But I've played the fool a time or two.

The plot thickens
Now in days it seems that self-respect is missing
Maybe it's the lack of being Christians
Or parents raising kids with tainted visions
You are a shining star, a blooming rose
Unlimited possibilities on how far you can go
You just must believe in yourself
If you can't do it, then why would anyone else?

Pride

The more I try, the less I understand
You rather die with dignity, than live feeling less of a man
You never back down from anything
No matter how wrong you can be
And you want me to stand beside you when you act a fool
My common sense won't allow me to
Pride will have you dead in a ditch
And sometimes the fight isn't even worth it.

Backstabber

My mom warned me that these females are nothing but phonies
And my dad told me, "Sex will turn men into dummies"
How do he go from filet mignon to bologna?

What was crazy about it, is that you were my best friend since age 8
We went from double-dutch to double dates
It's ridiculous how a man came in the way
But I can't deal with you no more, so now I have to skate
Because you are so fake, backstabbing, and two-faced.

You kept telling me to leave
You said "Don't stay, girl you can do better anyways"
You said he was treating me wrong
Now you are laying in his arms
Talking about you didn't mean to hurt me
I'm not trying to hear that broken song
Now I am on my own— but so long.

It's crazy how y'all did this behind my back though
But you know how the saying goes
What goes around, then back around it will go
The dark always finds its way back into the light you know
The lights are now on, and you've been exposed
There is no need for hiding
I can see your true colors shining.

Desperation

It's blatantly disrespectful how you make your intentions known
You see this ring on my finger, and you see him on my arm
Yet you still go to all extremes to try to have him as your own
Taking indecent measures to break up our happy home
Even though his undying love for me is evidently shown.

I'm on this throne and I won't give it up
We've been through too much to let these haters ruin us
It seems everywhere I go I get envious looks
Yes he is mine, and you won't take him from me like crooks
I see how you eyeball my man, as if I am not standing next to him
I see the jealousy in your eyes, the hunger every time we walk by
You're a nickel and I'm a dime, why would he waste his time?

It's scandalous how they do this underneath my nose
Hoes, find a man of your own, and leave mines alone
He don't want you and I'm not insecure— that is not the issue
It's just rude and you look pitiful.

It's obvious that you are desperate
Aren't you tired of being the other chick?
Aren't you tired of secondhand penis?
You are home-wrecking red-handed
You need to up your standards.

You knew he was married, and now you act as if you had no clue
And if you do succeed, then you would be the fool
Because if he cheats on me, he'll do the same to you
But if he does choose to bang you, then you did me a favor
Because I don't need a man that is weak natured.

Poor Rich Girl

Meet Kim, she was my friend since age 10
She had a rich family, with big plans,
and her whole life in her hands
While we were playing in the sand
Her uncle would be playing in her pants.

I knew something was different
It's like her soul went missing
I'm sure he took it with him
He wanted to take us fishing, he kept pushing me to go
And she kept telling me no
But back then I didn't understand, now I know
He was trying to get my soul, but she wouldn't let him, though.

That was 10 years ago, and the abuse took a toll
So much to live for, but she can't let it go
Imagine her sorrow, with a pill too hard to swallow
Insides she's so hollow, so she turns to the bottle
It's hard to cope with life when your mom is doped up, right?
And your uncle is on top of you, what is a 12-year-old to do?
She turns 22 with the same issues, and same abuse.

She is the same girl, but now so lost in this world
She was molested as a child, now she's all buck wild
She stays drunk in the club, showing every dude love
Now she hates herself
She has no inner wealth, just thinner health
I tried to help her, and she burned me
She screamed, "Don't Judge Me!"

Life has got her beat
She is in her early twenties, but she could pass for forty-three.

She reeks of whiskey and weed,
and she is expecting her third seed
Just to think if she hadn't have saved me,
this could have been me!

She keeps finding worthless men, that keep hurting her again
She feels so alone, as she has a house, but has nowhere to call home
This can't be life at all
She's five feet trying to walk tall.

That's how the circle of life goes
But we must break this cycle
We need to look to the bible,
while we are on this yellow brick road
Because what's all the riches and golds,
if you don't have your soul?

I tried to tell her, but she wouldn't listen
I gave her a bible, and said, "Become a Christian"
I said "Instead of turning to Rob, you should be turning to God."

She responded, "God doesn't exist,
If he did, then why am I living like this?
You don't know what I been through
Remember, I saved you!
But where was my hero? I needed one too!"

"You don't know my struggle, you don't know my pain
All you see is trouble, all I see is shame
Do you know that I feel hate every time I look at my son's face?
Because in his eyes, I see the man responsible for my rape.
That man took away my faith
You had a childhood, I didn't, mine was taken away
He told me if I told anyone then I was as good as dead
That will mess up a child's head."

"Do you know what it's like to be jealous of your own daughter?
Or how about growing up with no father?

My only father figure abused me since I was a toddler
And I don't even want to talk about my train-wreck of a mother
You say pray, but why bother?
I was born into rich scum; how come?
I'm living proof that you can have the hugest trust funds,
But without guidance and love, you're just a poor rich bum."

I couldn't pretend to understand her pain
But I told her, "With God, there so much you can gain
He wouldn't have given you life, for you to throw it down the drain
He died for our sins, so don't let that be in vain
It's not too late to change
You need to seek professional help
If you can't do it for yourself, then do it for your children's health
They need a hero too, and first it starts with you
Do you want them going through what you've been through?
I can't walk in your shoes
But I can tell you, when you walk against God, you'll always lose.
Your kids may see your drunk mother when they look at you
This cycle has to end, and that is something only you can do."

Written as a reflection of observed struggles, not as a factual account. Dedicated to resilience and hope for those who suffer.

Hard Times

There is no love in this frigid world
Just slugs that consistently hug
Even your own blood will give you up for a dub
Sink or swim in this ocean and we are all floating
Popping pills and potions until we're overdosing
Everyone is living life in slow motion and barely coping.

It seems most people can't get by without getting high
Either on perks, mollies, and china white, or Kush and purple sprite
It's because of the high life, that's one of the reasons we love life
Most people can't function without a substance
Or they will malfunction without the loving—isn't that something?

Even lawyers and doctors, or politicians and scholars
Those with white collars or blue
These are the hard times we go through
Life has you shook, this isn't Never-Ever Land
We have real Captain Hooks, and you are no Peter Pan
Think fast because you must have a plan
Your time is near the end when you are living in this quicksand.

Lately it seems death wants to meet me
It's too often someone close leaves me
I don't get enough time to weep
Sporadically my heart beats
So, before I go to sleep I have to say my prayers
We are living in the world of nay-sayers
Where nothing is fair, and no one cares.

Most people are just living to die
It's an eye for an eye and a tooth for a tongue
We do onto others what others have done.

Life is not perfect
Some are halfway in Hell trying to grasp the surface
But I will prevail
Life has us hooked like fish scales.

Many men wish death on me
But many men aren't blessed as me
It's no surrender, no retreat
I have asthmatic rhymes, with every line it's hard to breathe
I'm steadily gasping for air
Holding onto my cross, "Lord are you still there?"
I'm alive so of course He's here
So that means no other shall I fear.

Break These Chains

Trapped by pain, held down by fear,
Every link a wound from the past I still hear.
But even iron cannot hold my spirit,
Strength breaks what fear created—
I am free, I am unbroken.

The shadows whisper, but they cannot stay,
Each sunrise calls me to a brighter day.
The weight I carried has lost its claim,
No chain can bind what hope has named.

I rise from ashes, scars made new,
Living proof of what faith can do.
No burden heavy, no night too long,
My voice returns, my soul is strong.

These chains are no longer mine to carry,
Love and light are what I marry.
Fear may linger, but it will fade,
For I am stronger than what was made.

These chains can no longer weigh me down—I am renewed.
Now I walk with purpose, carrying a new attitude.
I've arrived, so blessed to be alive,
And finally, I'm loving the person inside.

I am free, I am unbroken.
I have broken these chains.

Dreams

Don't just go through life—
Grow through it.
Your dreams are close, just stay persistent.
Stand tall when you stumble,
With broken wings, you still fly.
Even when terrified, you must still try.

Keep moving, keep your stride—
Only the strong survive.
But strength is more than muscle;
It's faith when you're fragile,
Hope when you're humble,
And courage when the world says no,
While you keep moving forward, refusing to fumble.

The sun don't shine—
It just rains and pours.
But keep your head up,
Keep reaching for more.

They can't take us from our dreams.
They can't break us from our dreams.
They can't shake us from our dreams.
We are stronger than it seems.

Don't stop—dreams don't vanish.
They grow stronger; they will not banish.
Rise with them when you step to the fight,
What feels impossible today
Becomes tomorrow's light.

God loves you still,
Even if nobody else will.
And when the world whispers quit,
I hear Him shouting rise.
The sky is the limit,
A reminder that glory survives.

Everything is not what it seems—
So continue to follow your dreams.
Keep your eyes open,
Your plans in motion,
And your spirit unbroken.
You are living proof:
Dreams do come true.

Life's not perfect, but it's worth it.
So keep working—whether you're in college or raising kids.
From barbers to surgeons, we all have a purpose.
Keep searching, steer clear of the serpents.
I've barely scratched the surface,
But I've already touched my first wish—
And in these pages, my dream lives.

Facing Demons

You won't let me live in peace
Constantly haunting me
Following me every step I take
Every move that I make
You are constantly over my shoulder
Putting on so much pressure like a 3-ton weight
I can no longer keep my composure
I can't hold on to you any longer
Please go away!

I thought I buried you in the past
But you keep coming right on back
I thought I got rid of you
But when I look in the mirror, you are constantly there
Once again haunting me— and taunting me
Suffocating me until I can no longer breathe
Please go away!

I am a better person today
I have matured and grown to be an amazing woman
But again you won't let me live in peace
Constantly tossing and turning in my sleep
When I awake you are still there
Next to me, stroking my hair
Please go away!

You are driving me insane
Taking me to a dark place
A place I never want to relive again
I was told in order to break from you
I must face you head on
So I get the strength to stand against you.

So that I can be free from these memories
And I can look in the mirror one day and see the new me
I will no longer have to hide
Because there's no longer demons that live inside
They went away!
And now I'm free to be me!

Time is Ticking

I've done everything right, everything in order
I went to school and got two degrees
I'm drug, alcohol, and debt free
I'm successful in terms of a career
But it's my personal life that's in arrears.

So many people my age have done things backwards
They had kids at a young age, and careers are below average
Some have been married and divorced
I have not been married or had any kids, so which one is worse?
To have it and struggle or fail, or to never have experienced it at all
All my life, I thought if I did things right and in the correct order
Then I would reap the benefits of a husband—
and a son or a daughter, not just a baby father.
I've purposely waited to have children, as I wanted marriage first
Now my biological clock is ticking, and I feel like I'm being cursed
What am I to do?

I'm dating a great man, we've only been together for a few months
He has two kids and was married once
At some point he had everything that I want
He wants to be together a couple of years before marriage
But first he is willing to give me the baby and the carriage
The problem is I always wanted everything done the right way
If I wanted just a child I would have had a baby already
But if I wait for marriage, I may not be able to have a child
Because it's a process to get to know someone and get to that point
And I don't have that time now.
Time is not on my side, and I am on a mission
The biological clock is ticking
I have to choose between marriage and children
It's not fair that everything I control I have made a huge success.

But the one thing I can't control is making me a mess
I hate depending on someone else, that's something I never do
Why do I have to be dependent to make my dreams come true?
We depend on men to propose at the right time
So everything else can fall in line.
Men don't have these issues, they can be forever fertile
But for me to get what I want, I have to jump over hurdles
I don't want to settle, but I am in dire need for a biological child
I must decide soon, because my time is running out.

Dependency

For the longest, you always needed a pick-me-up to get by
It's sad that every time I see you, you're either drunk or you're high
I know life can get tough
But you can't let yourself self-destruct.

I remember as kids we said everything we'll never do
We'll be good parents, successful, and drug-free too
Now look, you're everything you said you wouldn't be
When you're young, I understand, but now you're 33
Please get it together, I'm rooting for you
I'm missing the joyful person I once knew.

You think it makes you better, but it doesn't
In this world, a good portion of people are dependent
They couldn't function daily without a substance
Without it, they wouldn't know what to do with themselves
When you get to that point, then you need help.

What are you going to do, take pills all your life?
That can't be right
At some point your body will give up the fight
Then you'll move onto stronger things to chase that high
It's a gateway, and you're already inside.

Parents, be careful what you're giving your kids
I know these behavior disorders can be ridiculous
But stimulants can be very addictive
No substance should ever have anyone dependent
Some of the side-effects are worse than the problem
When you lose your personality, do these pills really solve them?

I've seen people go from energetic to zombie mode
It's sad watching someone you love in that zone
If the good outweighs the bad, then I understand
But some people are just blowing in the wind
Once you start messing with their brain
Some people will never be the same.

Angels

The older I get, the more people I lose
So I want to be young forever
My heart has succumbed to the pain
And remains numb
For my heart is a casualty of love and life
Afraid to love anyone new
Because that'll be more pain I endure
When I have to mourn another loss.

It's sad to say that I'm used to death
Because everyone around me leaves
Afraid of living life to the fullest
Because failure is always lurking over my head
It seems I get punished for just living
I have to keep pushing, even when I can no longer finish
But I'd rather put forward my best effort
Than not try at all.

My angels surround me daily
They make sure I never fall
Although I lost you in flesh, you are always in my heart
Angels are there every step of the way
From your accomplishments to your darkest days
Shielding you from harm and pain
Being your umbrella when it rains.

R.I.P. Angels

Jasiah Dudley	Ernestine Thompson	Deborah Hickinbottom
Geraldine Oden	Walker Herman Oden	Joel Hickinbottom Jr.
Thomas Ferguson	Tomisha Gilcreast	Donna Crockett
Hollie Jackson	Tim Boucher	Fabo
Shay Jordan	Raymond Wise	Ruth Nieves
Dwayne Farmer	Trisa Otero	Devin Thompson
Karen Johnson	Matthew McClary	Kristina Powell
Joel Hickinbottom Sr.	Shirley Butler	Darrell Brian Butler
Ian Kelley	Kasheif Turner	Eddie Malave
Brianne Chadwick	Lisa Clark	Gerald Clark Sr.
Steven Stokes	Heath Ward	Kerringten Wright
Sara Hernandez	Marylyn Blake	Samuel Abrams

Safe Place

Through it all, God is always with me
Leading me, comforting me
And keeping me safe no matter where I am
This is important to know
Because life can be very difficult at times for kids my age.

For kids my age, safe places are everything to us
Three places we should feel safe at are at home, school, and church
But that's not the case for most kids anymore
It is sad when your safe places are no longer safe anymore
Because some crazy person with a gun has something to prove.

A lot of kids don't feel safe anywhere, anymore
Especially when there's church shootings
because of their skin color
Can we not even feel safe in our own skin, anymore?
Some are afraid to leave home because of shadows of brutality
So, do you see how it can be hard for someone like me?
For someone my age?
For someone my race?
Someone just witnessing and soaking all this in.

I'm not even a pre-teen
I must worry about escape routes, and learn to hide from danger
Most kids won't understand what it is to be safe
And most would give up and just go the other way
But I don't let those devils affect me
No obstacles will stand in between God and I
Because I know with God, all things are possible.

With God all things are possible
And that is why I am still alive.

That is why my head is always held high
And that is why I always have a smile on my face
Because I know God will always protect me, and keep me safe.
Where there is God, there is a way
Only God controls my heart or my fate
God is the president of my life
So, with God, all things are possible!

I said, with God, all things are possible!
That's why I just focus on what I can control
God will take care of the rest
I focus on being a great person inside and out
I focus on getting good grades, loving myself, and my family
I focus on praying daily, and going to church weekly
I focus on these things, because that's all I need
When God has you, He is more than enough.

God is all I need; can you say the same?
Nothing else matters, because God will provide for you
God will keep you unscathed
God will take care of your mind, body, and soul
So, there will be no need to fear anyone
Or to fear going anywhere
Because God is your safe place.

With God in your life and in your heart, you are safe anywhere
Just remember with God, you can be and do anything you desire
There are no ceilings when the sky is the limit
You can only succeed higher, and further
When you follow the path God led you to
And with God, all things are possible!

This piece is written in the imagined voice of a child. It is a work of creative expression, highlighting resilience and faith rather than literal events.

Robbed

I was robbed last night
At 9:38 pm to be exact
I was drawing my bath, then I heard a crash,
There he stood 6'2" in a mask
At 9:38 pm to be exact.

That was the time my most prized possession was ripped from me
I begged and pleaded, I screamed "NO!"
"Please stop! Please don't do this! Let me Go!"
He refused
In fact, my pain seemed even more of a turn-on
At 9:38 pm, I knew my soul was gone.

I could feel the cold knife on my neck
I could feel the dripping of the sweat from his chest
I can still feel the bruises that he left
From him holding me down with all his might
Physically I am still alive
But mentally I died inside that night
Never will I be the same again
Never will I feel that pain again.

I was robbed last night
Robbed of my trust, robbed of my faith
Robbed of my love, robbed of my cake
You all don't understand how this destroyed my mental state
My body and mind were my temple, something that God built
Well, now my temple has been infested with evil and filth
That's what you left inside.

And it won't die with any pesticide
And no matter how many times I bathe
There's no cleanser that can wash that stench away.

9:38 — the last time I saw on that clock.
9:38 — the moment when time stopped.
9:38 — the second I died.
9:38 — the instant hate arrived.

9:38 — when you let your guard down.
9:38 — when your weapon hit the ground.
9:38 — when you thought I'd relax...
But I surrendered only to your ruthless attack.

That's when you believed you had my best.
9:38 — when I drove the knife through your chest.
9:38 — when you gasped your last breath.
9:38 — when we both met death.

But in flesh, I remain alive.

Rot. In. Hell.

Hands Off

You can't just take things that don't belong to you
Didn't your mom teach you such?
You can't just walk up and touch
That's how you'll end up in handcuffs.

You have to show respect to get it
There is no special privilege? — let's really inspect it.
You do the crime, you get the same sentence—
but somehow, justice still feels selective.
Just because she's dressed provocative, doesn't make her a slut
And if you think that makes it okay to rape her, then you're nuts.
You can't grab women by their *treasure box* and think it's justified
Would you think it was acceptable
if done to your daughter or wife?

Harassment or assault has no sex or race
So if anyone treats you inappropriately, put them in their place
We should feel secure in our careers without sexual advances
We shouldn't feel ashamed to stand up for ourselves in any instance
No means no, and if you go against that, you will pay the cost
So, to be safe, keep your inappropriate thoughts to yourself,
And most importantly, keep your hands off!

Strength

Do you even know your own strength?
Do you know how powerful you are?
A single mom who has raised 3 kids
Working 3 jobs to meet ends
And you are going to school online too
These kids are watching and looking up to you
They are proud of what you do
Never making up any excuse
You just put your mind and skills to good use
Not waiting for a hand-out
But not ashamed to take any
Your courage and strength stands out
Amongst a world where ambition is running empty.

Respect goes out to those still following their dreams
No matter what obstacles have come in between
There is beauty in those that don't settle
When life hands you the bronze, you go for the gold medal
No offense for those content with being basic
Or those that fell complacent
Just shining spotlight on those who strive for greatness
Those that set goals and are still chasing them
Those that are aware that we lead by example
Only the strong survive, the weak gets dismantled
You're a star, don't you forget it
The universe will soon align, and you'll reap all the benefits.

Resilience

In a world where some people are puppets of Satan
They claim freedom is given, yet it's often forsaken.
My choices must align with the morals I've been taught
Navigating paths where righteousness is sought.
With these broken wings I learned on my own to fly
In hopes that I pick the path that's right.

It seems friends hurt you quicker than your enemies
Never wear your heart on your sleeve
It gives others easy access to inflict pain
In a society where the normal is to be insane.

I was once scared
I was on the road to nowhere
But who the hell cared?

I'm just a diamond in the rough
I don't know if it's the love or the slugs
The blood or the hugs
It's a thin line between the good and the bad
I made riches from rags
And I didn't have to sell one bag.

Addicted

I wish you would love me more than you love that bottle
We'd still be together if that was the case
I loved you through thick and thin
But my identity was being erased.

I didn't like who I was becoming with you
Your broken promises kept me frustrated and confused
I was acting out of character daily
I needed to step back because darkness was taking over me
You would upset me and I wouldn't handle it well
I had to choose a life without you, or going to jail.

My darker side was beginning to surface
So I had to walk away so I could live with a purpose
The alcohol made you different and as a result I changed too
Through rehab and hospitalizations, I supported you
I wanted to help you get better and fight for us too
But you were having difficulty pushing through
I kept praying this relapse would be your last time
But you took me on an emotional rollercoaster ride.

I did the best I could
But it was never good enough
13 years down the drain, but I can't keep feeling stuck
You drained me dry
Physically, emotionally, financially— I have no more tears to cry
I wish I could have saved you from yourself
But for my sanity, I had to worry about myself.

I was embarrassed, dealing with an addict
Constant withdrawals, then you went right back at it
I would lie to those around me, pretending I was fine.

Like your problem wasn't extremely out of line
But being in denial does not give you peace of mind.

I wish you would love me more than you love that bottle
Because you were my soulmate
We had plans for a baby and we set a wedding date
And it's a shame that I had to step away
I can no longer stay in a place where I don't feel safe.

Bench Press the Sky

There are limits — but even they can be lifted beyond the sky.

They stacked the world on my chest —
The doubts, the fears, the failures —

Each weight a whisper:
"You're not strong enough."
"You'll never rise."

All pressing down like iron plates.

But I refused to suffocate beneath the weight.
With trembling hands, I reached for more,
And pressed until my spirit roared.

Every rep became a prayer,
Every breath, a declaration:
I will not be crushed.
I will rise.

The world may try to pin me down,
But I was built to defy gravity.
Not just to lift the weight of my pain,
But to bench press the sky.

They said I'd break —
That pressure would shatter me into silence.

But I turned pain into power,
And fear into fuel.

I carried the weight, but I carried me too.
I am not your statistic.
I'm the exception.

The underdog that overachieved,
the storm they never saw coming.
I carved strength from struggle,
stitched faith into every fracture.

I don't just carry the weight —
I lift it.
I don't just dream —
I live it.

And every time life tries to press me down,
I press back harder —
Until the sky itself moves.

Watch me.
I was born to rise.

We only get one life, one try.
No rewind, no redo — just now.
They counted me out, but can't fit my crown.
I'm one of one, can't make me twice.
Forget just a slice —
I want the whole pie.
Whipped cream. The whole nine.
I will go for what's mine.

And I won't just touch high —
Watch me bench press the sky.

Unity

We are not the sum of what broke us.
We are the story of what survived.
The pain didn't bury us —
It planted something that still thrives.

There is light inside each scar,
And strength behind each tear.
What was meant to silence us
Only made our voice more clear.

They tried to dim our fire,
To divide us, erase our name.
But we rose from the ashes
With hearts still full of flame.

Not just as one —
But side by side.
Wounds may differ,
But our will is aligned.

Love is louder.
Hope is stronger.
Faith goes further
Than fear ever could wander.

We are not what we lost —
We are what we kept.
Our dreams.
Our truth.
The promises time never forgets.

So take my hand.
Lift your chin.
You are not alone.
You were never less than.
You are light.
You are love.
You are a reason to rise again.
From casualties to conquerors — we rise.
United by pain, yet empowered by purpose.

Touchless Existence

A force had come to try to get rid of love
Something that won't allow us to touch
No displays of physical affection
No hugs, no kisses, no caressing
It is trying to come in between love!

It has created a world where everyone must be 6 feet apart
You may take my space, but you can't take what's in my heart
We can't even see our families without fear of bringing them harm
I haven't seen my mom in months, this separation is hard.

Some people can't survive it
Just the thought of being alone has many dying
Some need that personal attention for affirmation
Mental health is serious, and some don't have any patience.

It tried to come in between love
I can't remember the last time I hugged
But it won't win
We still have memories, we still have emotions
Our bond is too strong to break us apart
No distance will ever keep you out of my heart.

Invisible Enemy

Everything is chaotic,
Numbers rise, and people fall apart.
We cover our faces, wash our hands,
Still the storm keeps breaking hearts.

So many mistakes are being made,
Yet so many try their best to stay safe.
And still it doesn't seem enough—
The losses keep mounting day after day.

I pray for those on the front lines,
Risking their lives to save lives,
Fighting an enemy no eye can see,
Scrubbing and washing, weary but steadfast,
Still afraid of bringing the danger home.

That is their life right now—
A burden heavy, a cost unseen.
Not for glory, not for wealth,
but because compassion drives their deeds.

Their lives are worth more than the task,
Their spirits worth more than the fear.
This unseen battle has taught us all
To hold tighter to the ones we love,
To cherish every breath, every moment near.

It reminds us not to take life for granted,
To value the smallest things—
A smile, a touch, a shared embrace—
Because tomorrow is never promised.

And still they rise, though weary and worn,
Facing each day as if newly reborn.
Their courage is quiet, their sacrifice deep,
A promise the world must never forget to keep.
I'm beyond grateful for all they do for me,
Putting up their best fight against an invisible enemy.
May their struggle remind us, in night or in flame,
To live with compassion, not treat life as a game.

Their lives are not a game.

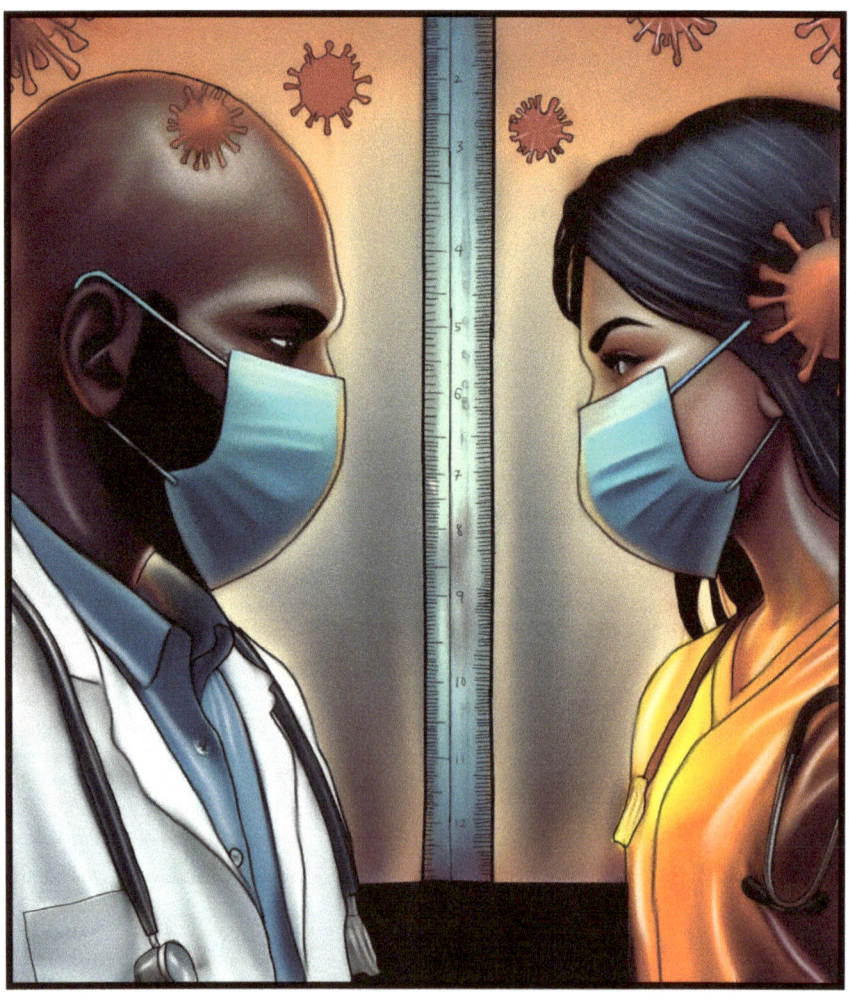

About Author

Alexis Quintia Oden grew up as a military dependent, living in many places across the United States, but she was primarily raised in North Carolina. She got her start in writing poetry at the young age of ten, honing her craft over the years. Writing poetry, books, short stories, and music has always been her passion. Her themes are love, life, heartbreak, faith, and loss. She earned her MBA in Business Management with certificates in Project Management and Healthcare Management at East Carolina University in NC. She is currently pursuing her doctoral degree while advancing her career in the business field. She will continue to write more books that promote self-worth and triumph. Oden's poetry offers a breath of fresh inspiration to every reader.

Instagram: @alexisqoden
X: @alexisqoden
Facebook: https://facebook.com/alexisqoden
Email: alexisqoden@gmail.com
TikTok: @alexisqoden
Website: www.alexisqoden.com

Illustrator Credits

Casualties of Love and Life features artwork commissioned under work-for-hire agreements and properly licensed visual assets. I extend heartfelt gratitude to the talented artists whose work visually enriches this collection.

Volontimir Gkasai / Vlad Gkasai Art (Vladimir Gasai) – Primary illustrator for the collection. Contributed more than 22 illustrations, including *Best Drug, Ice Box, Sullen Cries, Heartbroken, God's Love, Lover's Lane, Why Do You Hurt Me, Left for Dead, Forever Love, Wide Awake, Dark Clouds, Words Hurt Too, Whole Again, Self-Esteem, Mother Nature, Heat of the Night, Haters, Poor Rich Girl, Hard Times, Facing Demons, Angels,* and *Safe Place.*

Ayanfe Lawrence Bejide – Contributed seven illustrations: *Lifetime Friends, Prisoner's Song, Leap Love, Queen, Time is Ticking, Dependency,* and *Pandemic.*

Anthony Dudley – Contributed artwork for *Good Die Young and Our Saving Grace.*

Ranada Renee Williams – Contributed artwork for *Make Me Feel.*

HMDPublishing – Cover and interior design.

Adobe Stock – Provided supplemental imagery (*Angels* Artwork [Wings], Image ID #43727750, used under extended license).

Each contribution brought unique artistry that enhanced the spirit of this book.

www.ingramcontent.com/pod-product-compliance
Lightning Source LLC
Chambersburg PA
CBHW051621120626
46551CB00014B/1896